MAMA LOTTIES VEGAN COOKBOOK

Mama's 50 must-try vegan recipes

Recipes and photography copyright © Justin Bautista 2021
Mama Lotties Illustration by Amanda Richards
www.amandarichards.co.uk | @amandarichardsillustrations
Edited by Sophie Clifton-Tucker | www.sctcopy.com

The right of Justin Bautista to be identified as the Author of the Work has been asserted by him in accordance with the Copyright, Design and Patents Act 1988 in the United Kingdom and in accordance with the Intellectual Property (Copyright and Related Rights) Act 2005 Sections 94 and 95 in Gibraltar.

All rights reserved. No part of this publication may be reproduced, stored in a retrieval system or transmitted, in any form or by any means without the prior written permission of the publisher, nor be otherwise circulated in any form of binding or cover other than that in which it is published and without a similar condition being imposed on the subsequent purchaser.

ISBN   9798718349160

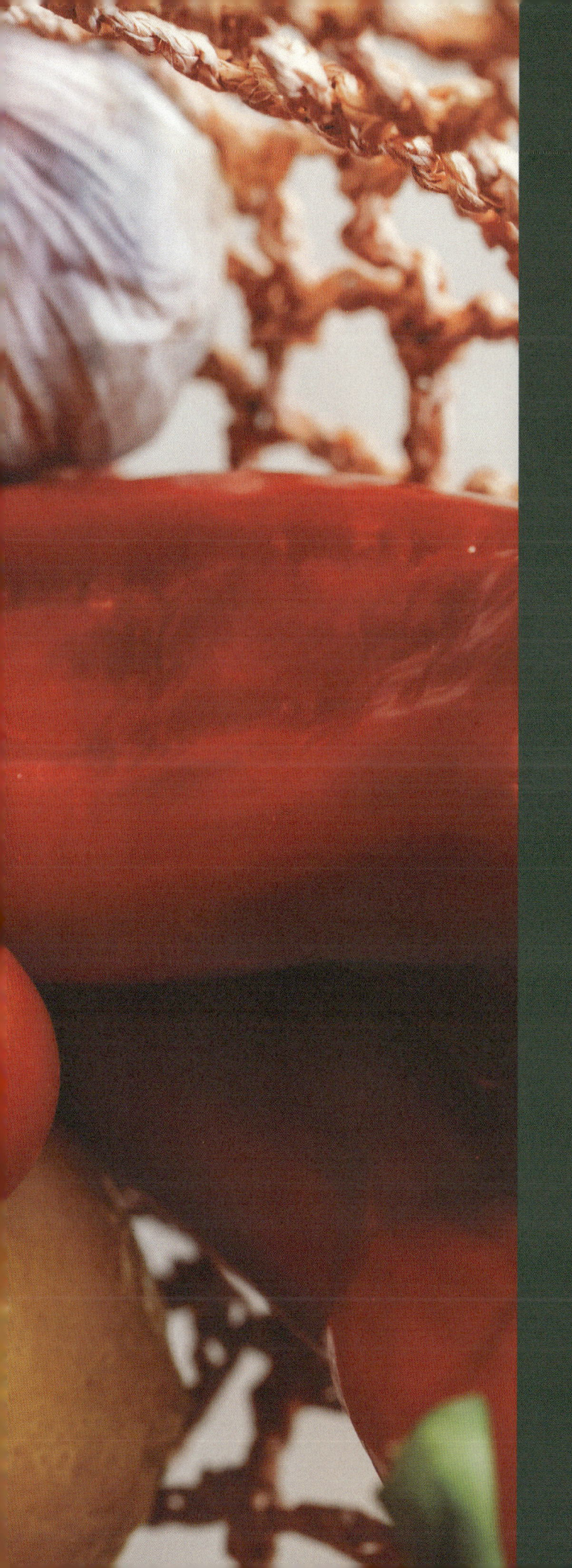

CONTENTS

THE INTRODUCTION

THE STARTERS

THE MAIN MEALS

THE SWEET TREATS

THE CAKES

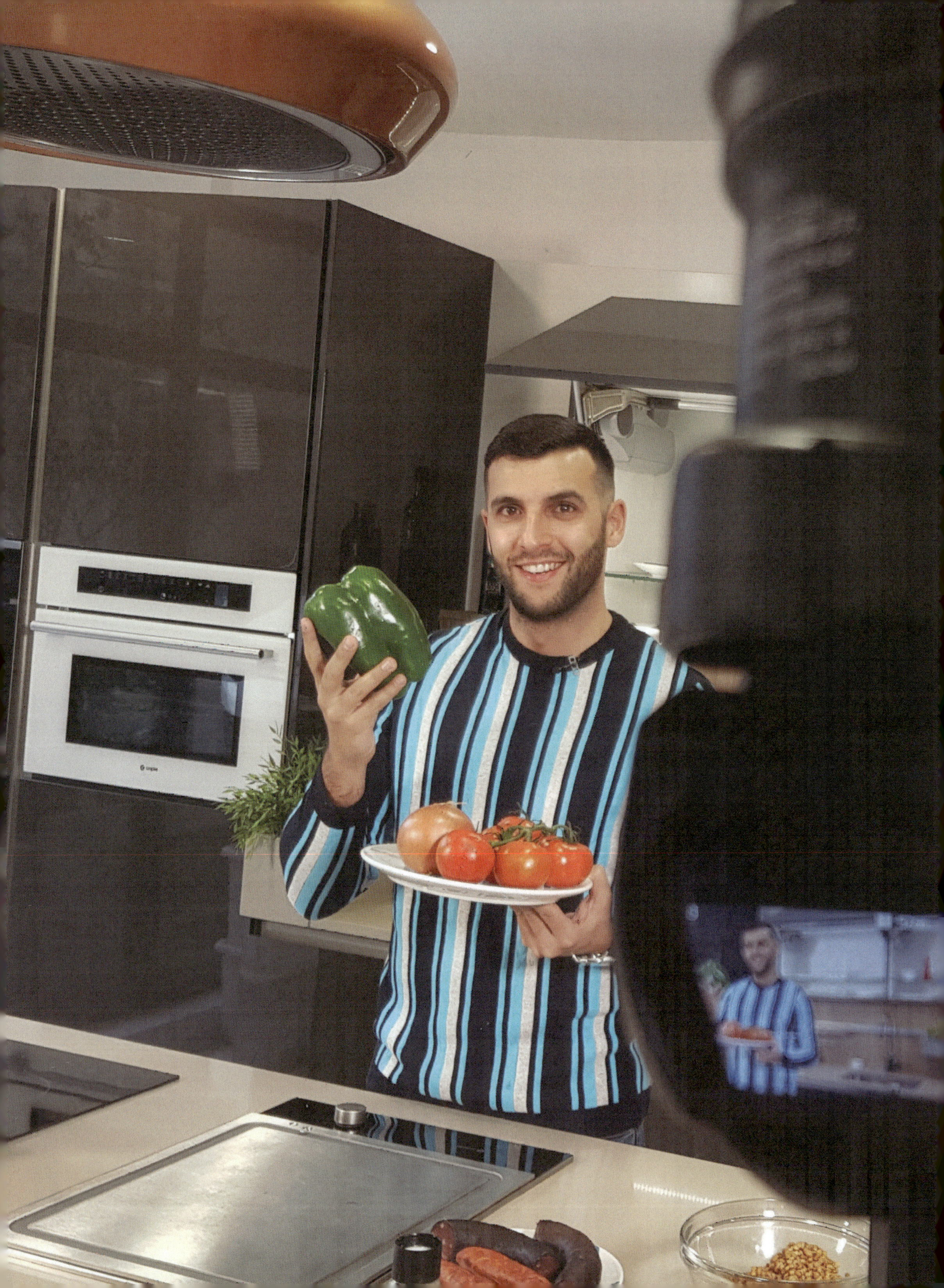

INTRODUCTION

I have wanted to put this book together for a long time now. My hope is that everyone can learn to enjoy cooking at home. Catering for vegans or those willing to add more vegan alternatives to their diets has been a goal of mine for several years.

Eating fresh and well does not have to be complicated. There are many things to be made with the everyday ingredients we find in our cupboards. What greater pleasure is there than to cook for yourself, or especially others, and enjoy a meal together knowing that what's in front of you has helped the environment around you?

Aside from fresh new recipes, my aim was to offer alternatives to the traditional Gibraltar favourites so that we may still connect and enjoy recipes we may have grown up with, now adapted to modern day life.

HAPPY COOKING! SHARE YOUR CREATIONS ONLINE WITH US AND TAG @MAMALOTTIES

What's in this book?
Discover the recipes...

The Starters

Oriental Floats

Roast Chickpea Bites

Beetroot Hummus

Cauliflower Bites

Olive Tapenade

Creamy Pumpkin Soup

Coconut Cream Drizzle Mint & Pea Soup

Ajoblanco (Cold Almond soup)

Cold Beetroot Soup (Chłodnik z botwinki)

Mushroom & Sweet Onion Pierogi (Dumplings)

Torta de Patata

Sour Cream

Torta de Acelga

The Main Meals

Sweet Potato, Chickpea & Spinach Pies

Vegan 'Cottage Pie'

Mixed Bean Taco

Lentil & Blackbean 'Meatballs'

Mama's Summer Black Bean Burgers

Mama's Minestra

White Sausage Broth

Mama's Lentejas (Lentil Stew)

Artichoke & Bean Stew

Sweet Potato, Chickpea & Spinach Coconut Curry

Bean & Cauliflower Green Curry

Yellow Mango Curry

Mama's Vegan Paella

Mushroom Stroganoff

Stuffed and Roasted Bell Peppers

Rigatoni with Aubergine & Black Olive Ragu

Sweet Potato Noodles & Red Pepper Sauce

Vegan Pad Thai

Creamy Mac & Cheese

Spaghetti Puttanesca

Spinach & Mushroom Ravioli

Mama's Vegan Rosto

The Sweet Treats

Banana Pancakes

Summer Berry Smoothie Bowl

Fudge Caramel

Chocolate, Avocado & Peanut Butter Mousse Pots

Chocolate Cookies

Coco Bars

Fruity 'Rocky Road'

Banana, Coconut & Chocolate Ice cream

Mama's Vegan Flan

Jam Biscuits

The Cakes

Bollos de Hornazo

Banana Bread

Carrot Cake with "Cream Cheese"

No-Bake Vegan Lemon Tart

Melt-In-Your-Mouth Chocolate Cake

Mama's Vegan Banoffee Pie

Replace those eggs!

Chia Seeds
1 tbsp + 80ml water

Liquid from Chickpeas
(Aquafaba)
Liquid from 400g jar chickpeas
(= 2 egg whites)

Ground Flaxseed
1 tbsp Flaxseed + 3 tsp water

Banana
Half a mashed banana

Agar
1 tbsp + 1 tbsp water

Avocado
50g mashed avocado

Peanut Butter
3 tbsp peanut butter

Pumpkin & Sweet Potato
25g pumpkin + 25g sweet potato
(both puréed)

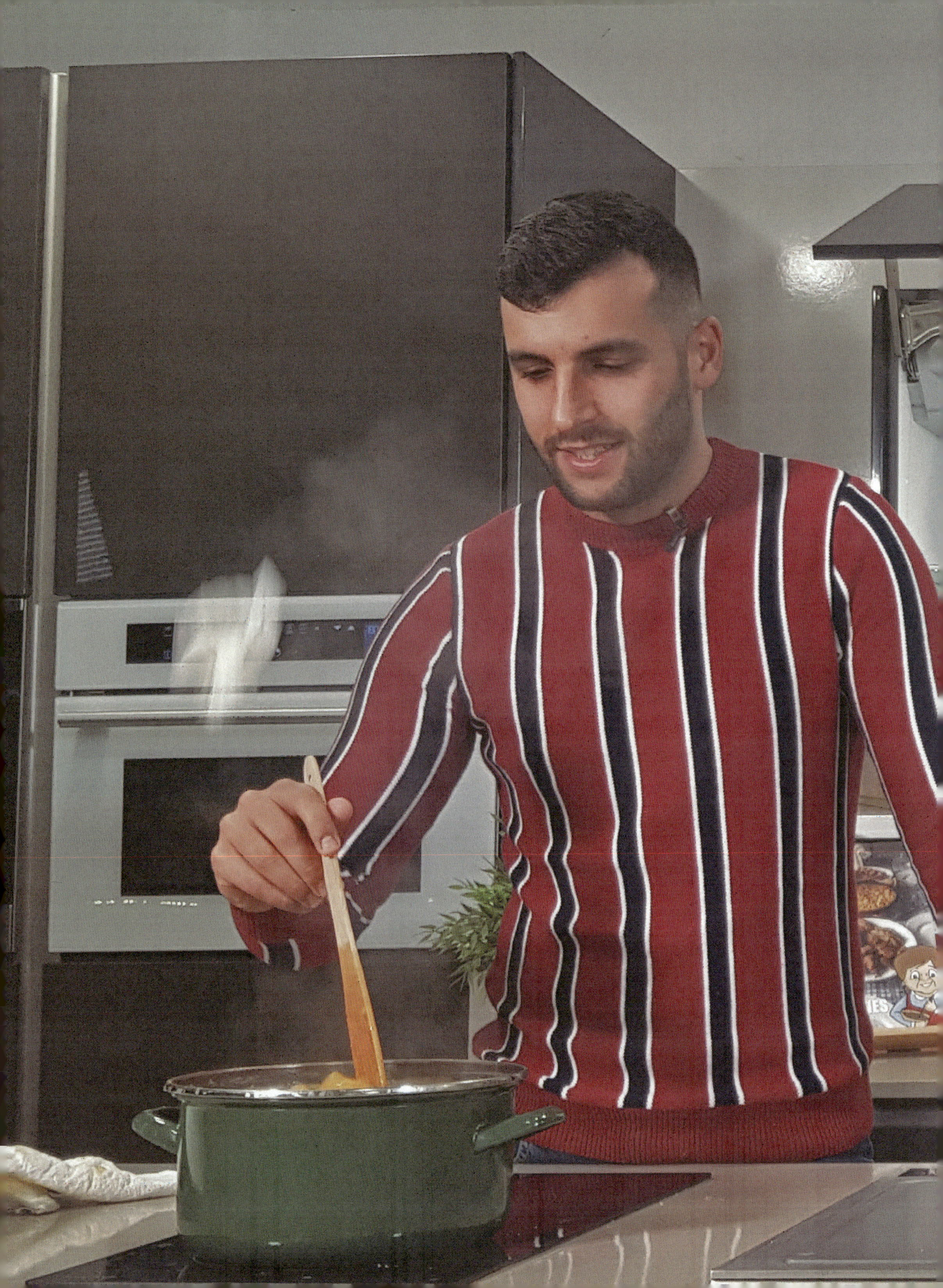

The Starters

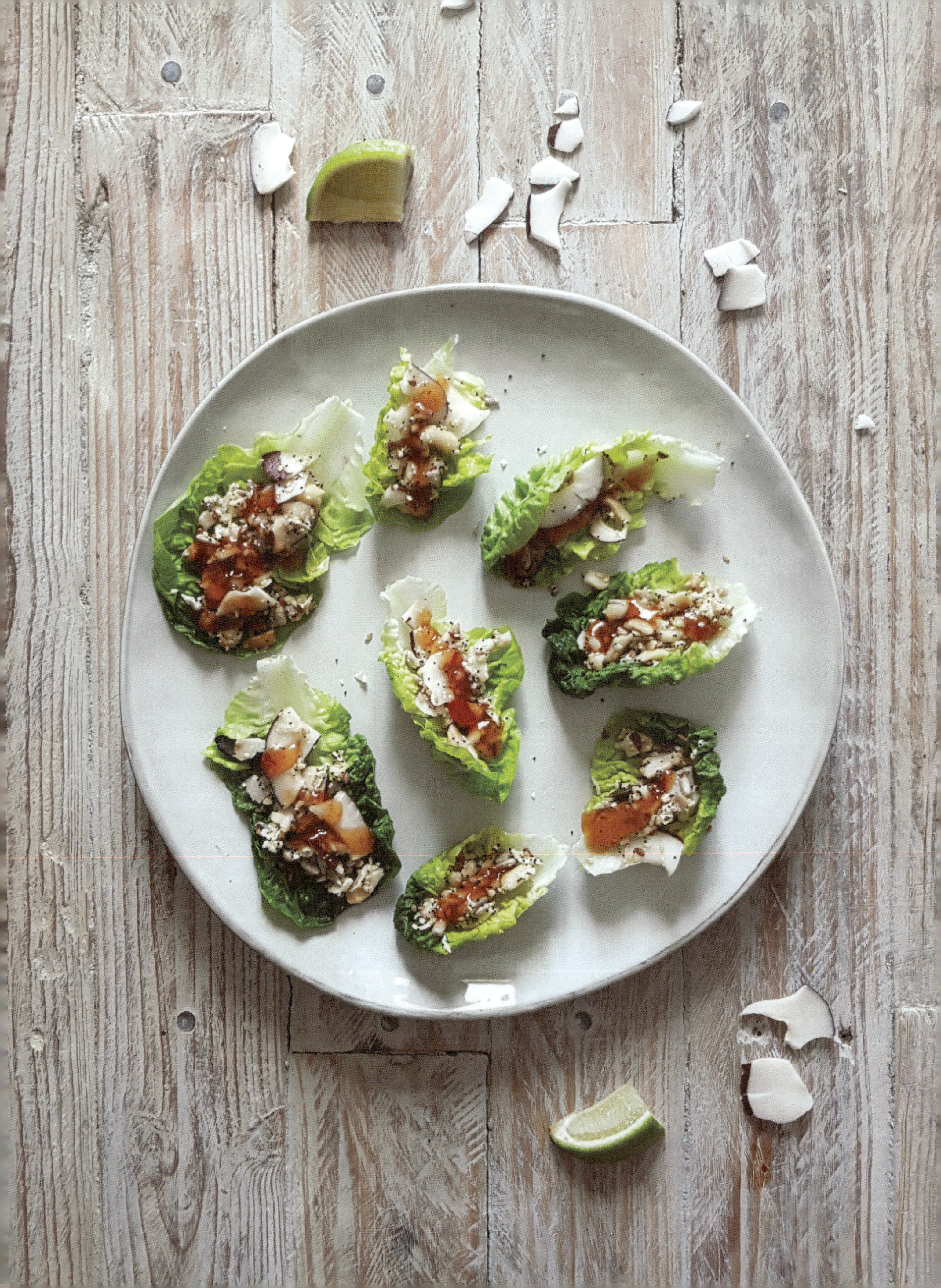

ORIENTAL FLOATS

Serves: 4 | Cooking Time: 20 Minutes

Snacks don't have to be just nuts or simple boring things. These oriental inspired floats are refreshing and also fun to make and serve to your friends.

INGREDIENTS

Baby lettuce leaves
Ginger root
1 lime
20g peanuts
20g pistachios
Toasted coconut
Sweet chilli sauce

TIME TO FEED THE SOUL

Peel back the baby lettuce leaves and wash them under running water. Chop any hard white ends leaving the leaves whole and open so that they act like boats. Put these to one side on a paper towel to drain.

Place the nuts in a small bag *(make sure to remove them from their shells first)*, and beat them until the nuts are crushed into small pieces.

Pour the crushed nuts into a bowl, remove the outer skin from the ginger root and grate the ginger over the nuts. Cut a lime in half and squeeze the juice on top. Finally, toss everything together.

Toast your coconut shreds in a pan over a high heat until the edges turn golden.

Now assemble the floats. Grab the lettuce leaves and lay them out individually, spoon some chilli sauce in the centre and the nut mix on top. Finally, sprinkle some of the toasted coconut over each float.

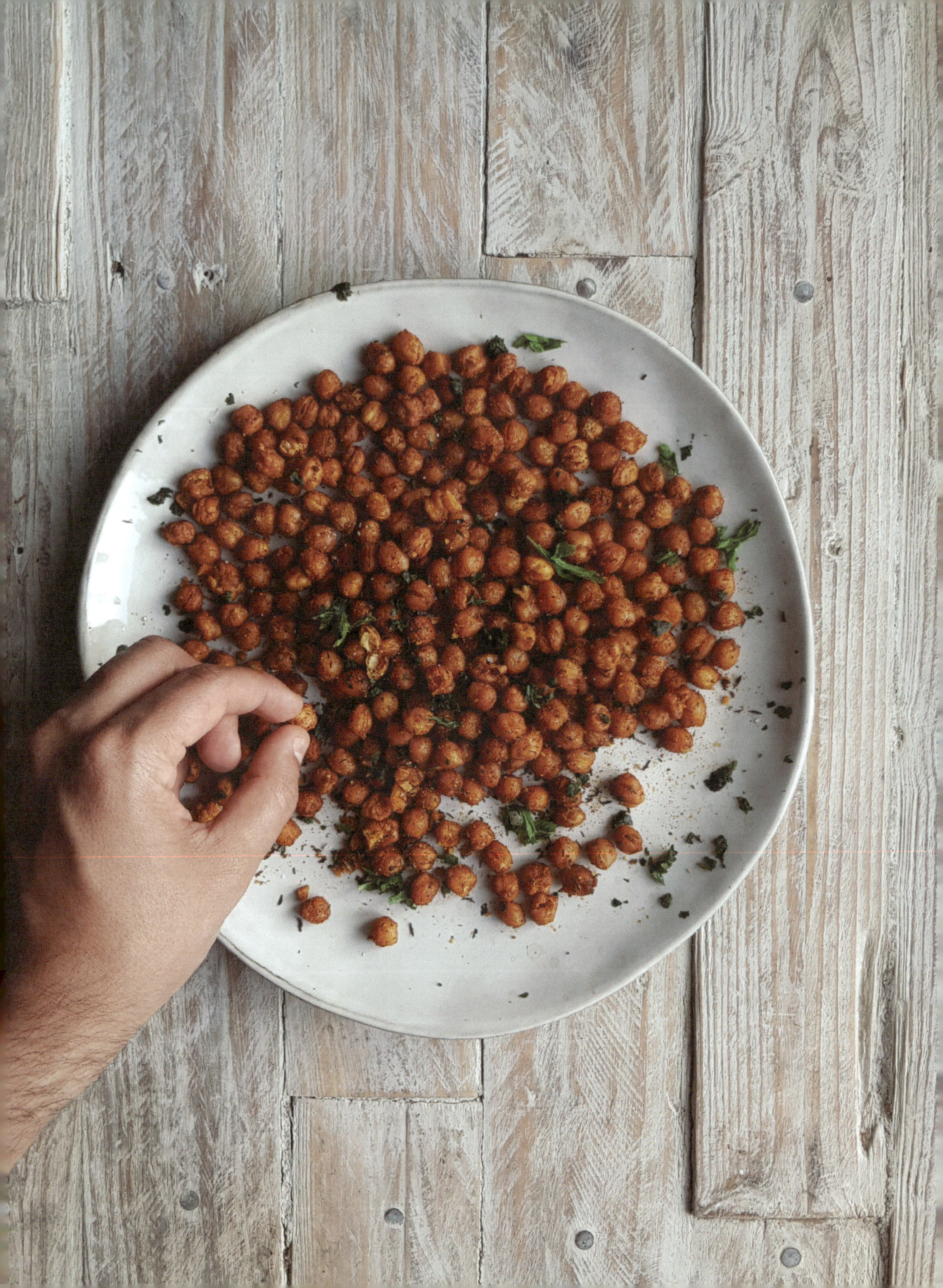

ROAST CHICKPEA BITES

SERVES: 3 | COOKING TIME: 50 MINUTES

Ever fancied a snack that you can take to the beach, enjoy hot or cold, or just nibble on while watching a movie? These roasted chickpeas are so simple to make and you can have them ready to eat in a jar to take with you.

INGREDIENTS

50g chickpeas *(soaked)*
Olive oil
Sea salt
1 tbsp smoked paprika
1 tbsp thyme
1 tbsp paprika
1 tsp chilli flakes

TIME TO FEED THE SOUL

What's important is to make sure you drain, rinse and dry your chickpeas out thoroughly. The best way to do it is to grab a clean kitchen towel and once you have rinsed and drained everything place them in the middle and pat them dry - just be careful not to squish them.

Place the chickpeas into a large bowl and coat them in a generous drizzle of olive oil, tossing them around inside the bowl with the herbs and spices to make sure you cover them all.

Turn the chickpeas out of the bowl onto a large baking tray, separating them so they're not too crowded together. Crack some salt over them all and put them in the oven at 150ºC for around 40 minutes, checking on them every 15 minutes or so to shake the tray. *(Be careful though as some may pop or spit.)*

Once that's done, transfer them into a bowl and toss them around with the seasoning.

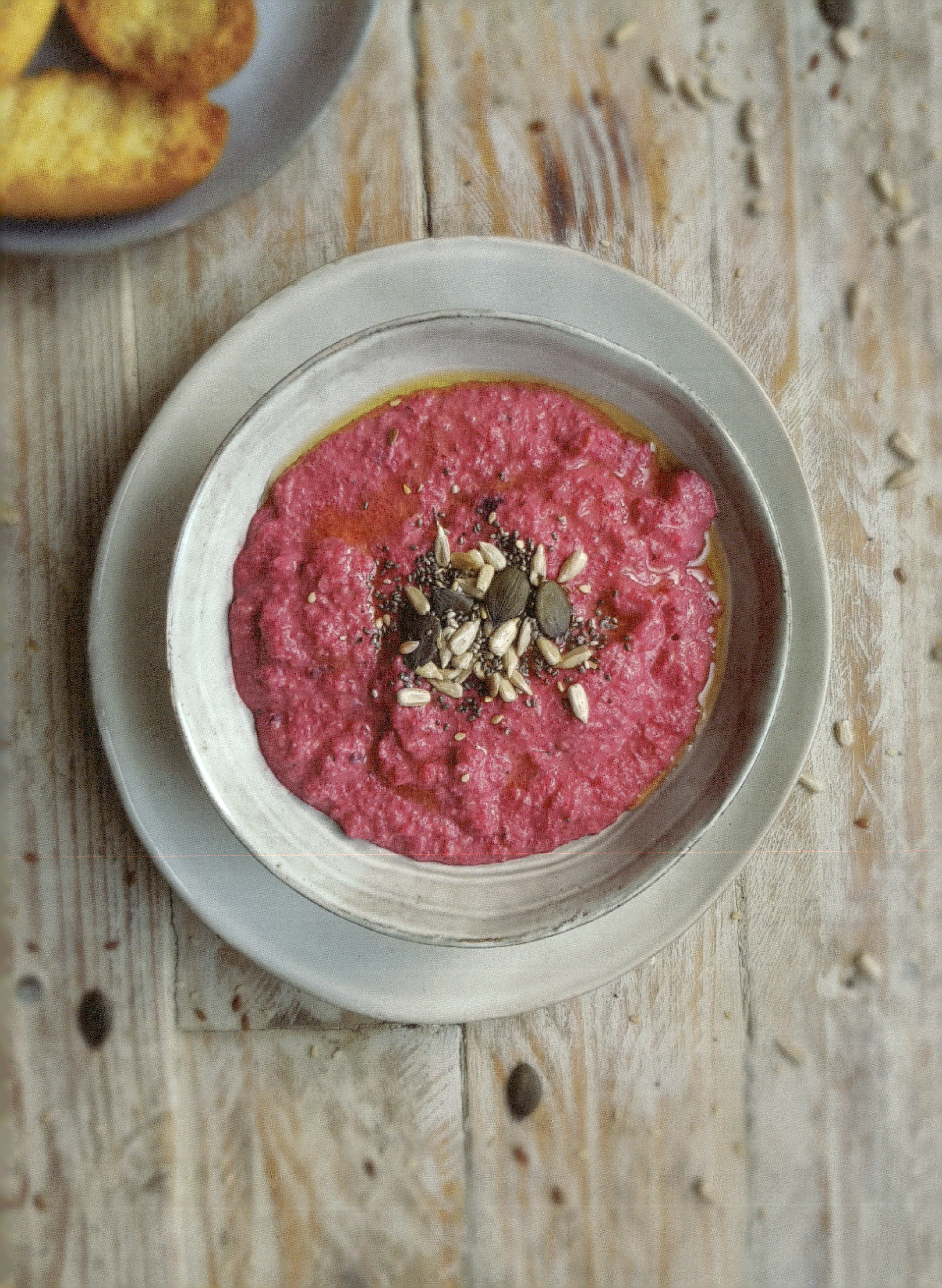

BEETROOT HUMMUS

SERVES: 3 | COOKING TIME: 10 MINUTES

Do yourself a favour and spoil yourself with some homemade hummus. There are so many different ways of making hummus, by which I mean different kind of ingredients you can use. Dip your favourite snacks in, or enjoy as a tasty starter.

INGREDIENTS

1 cooked beetroot
1 red onion
4 garlic cloves
400g jar drained chickpeas
10ml virgin olive oil
Sea salt
Black pepper
Thyme
1 tbsp tahini sauce *(optional)*
Bag of small nut mix *(optional)* (Sunflower seeds, poppy seeds, pumpkin seeds etc.)

TIME TO FEED THE SOUL

Crush the garlic, slice the onions and place them on an oven tray. Drizzle with oil, season with salt, pepper and thyme and leave under a medium to high grill for 5 - 10 minutes until soft and charred.

Pour the rest of the ingredients into a food processor with the other ingredients. Blitz together until you have a creamy purée, then include the onions and garlic.

Pour in the olive oil as you blend the ingredients. Transfer over to a nice bowl and serve with a drizzle of oil on top and if you want to, you can sprinkle a mix of nuts on top, though the nuts are optional.

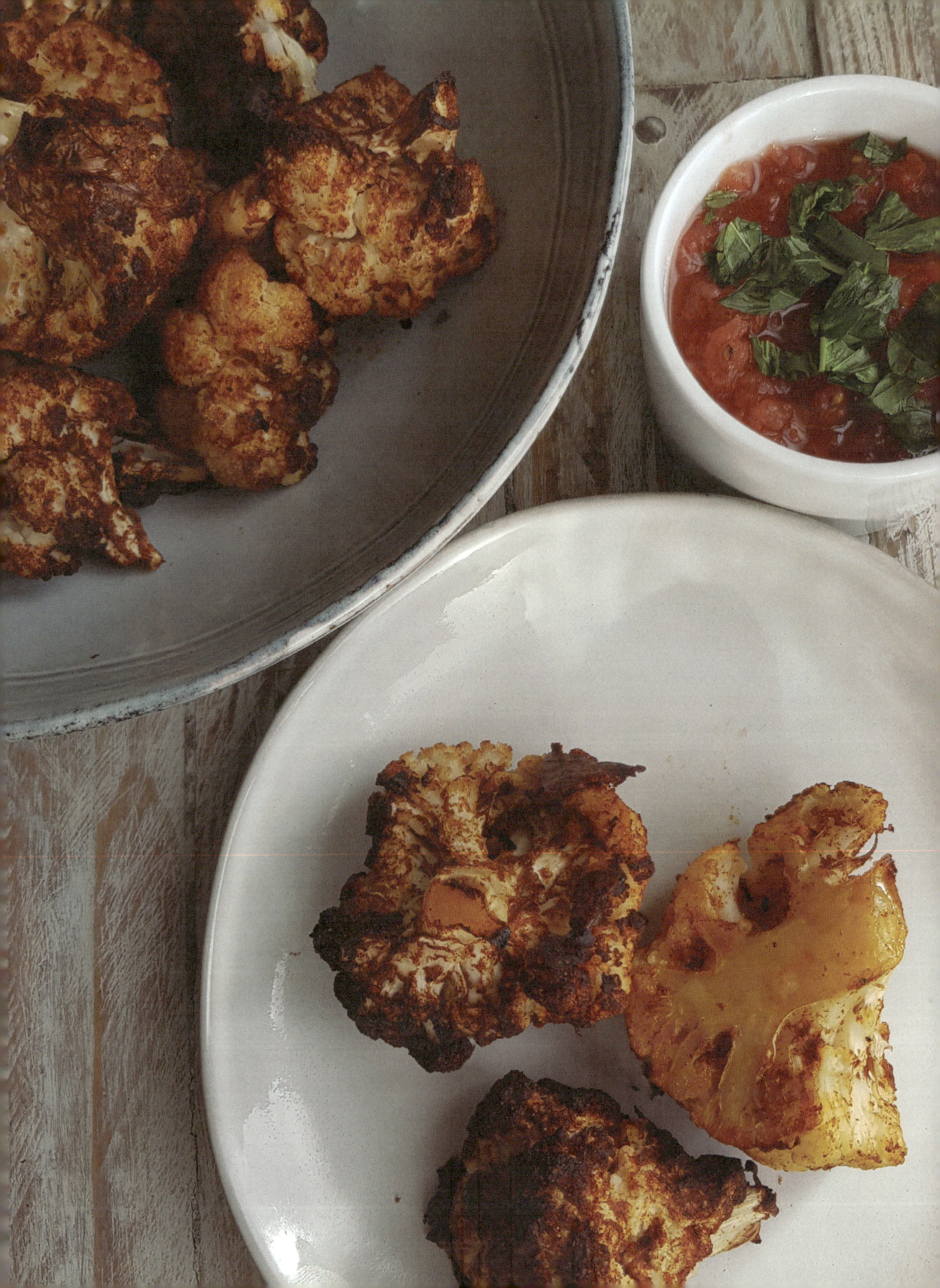

CAULIFLOWER BITES

Serves: 4 | Cooking Time: 30 Minutes

The alternative to BBQ wings, the meaty cauliflower and delicious seasoning, all marinated and combined together, then charred to perfection, makes this an ideal at home or BBQ dish.

INGREDIENTS

- 1 cauliflower head
- Olive oil
- 100g plain flour
- 2 tbsp sweet paprika
- 1 tsp cumin
- 2 garlic cloves
- 125ml almond milk
- Sea salt
- Black pepper

TIME TO FEED THE SOUL

Firstly, wash your cauliflower, then cut the leaves and ends off the cauliflower head and chop down the florets into smaller pieces.

In a bowl, mix all the remaining ingredients together (chopping the garlic down very fine) except the oil. Stir together into a paste. Dip your cauliflower into the paste and cover completely. Set aside.

Line a baking tray with greaseproof paper and lay the cauliflower on top, spaced out. Place the tray in the oven at 200ºC for 20 - 25 minutes. Remove the cauliflower from the oven and shake the tray, Drizzle with olive oil, lower the heat to 150ºC and bake for another 5 - 10 minutes.

When ready serve with some dip.

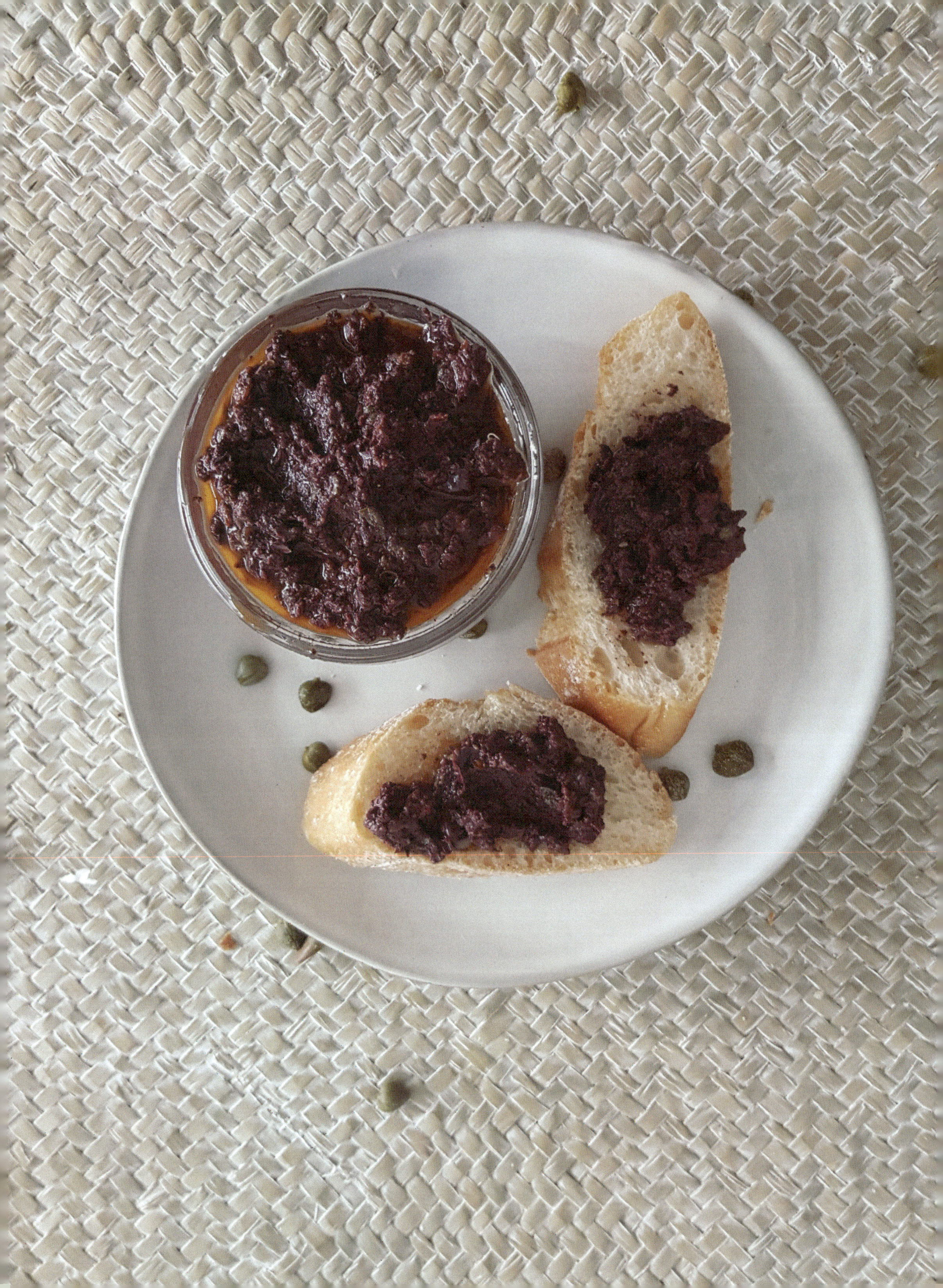

OLIVE TAPENADE

Serves 2 - 3 | Cooking Time: 5 - 10 Minutes

If you love olives as much as I do, you're in for a treat. The feeling of discovering another use for olives was pure delight as not only could I enjoy them for breakfast, but I could also spread it on pasta, or even use it as a dip! The kalamata olives are perfect as they are already very strong in flavour and naturally salty.

INGREDIENTS

- 300g - 400g black Kalamata olives
- 60ml olive oil
- 2 tbsp capers
- Juice of ½ lemon
- 2 - 3 garlic cloves
- 4 sun-dried tomatoes
- Black pepper

TIME TO FEED THE SOUL

Add all your ingredients into a food processor. We'll need to finely blend all the ingredients so that we have a smooth paste. *(Make sure you use olives without stones or remove them first.)*

Now it's up to you how smooth you want this paste. I like to have it smooth enough that you can butter it onto some bread or toast and enjoy it as a snack, like you would do with pate.

For a slightly sweeter version, roast or sauté your garlic, keeping them in their skin. Cooking the garlic makes them sweeter; then once they soften, remove them from their jackets and combine the cooked garlic into the paste to blend in.

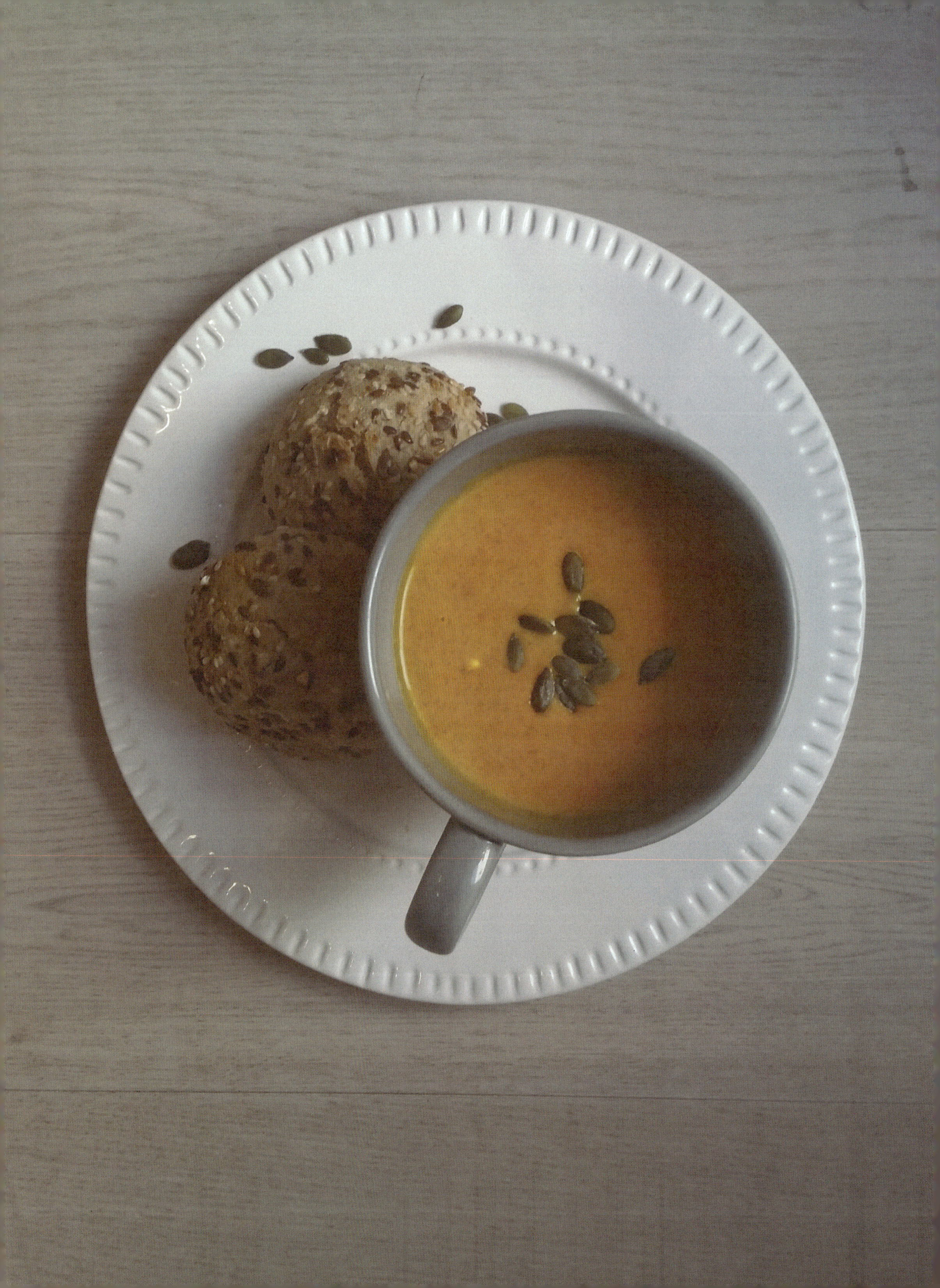

CREAMY PUMPKIN SOUP

SERVES: 5 | COOKING TIME: 1 HOUR

Pumpkins and autumn go together perfectly. When Halloween arrives make use of those pumpkins lying around and turn them into a creamy, soul comforting soup. This soup is sweet, smoky and oh so enjoyable.

INGREDIENTS

- ¼ pumpkin or butternut squash
- 400g frozen spinach
- 1 turnip
- 4 carrots
- 2 celery sticks
- 1 leek
- Garlic salt
- 200g vegan cream cheese
- Smoked paprika
- Olive oil
- 1 vegetable stock cube

TIME TO FEED THE SOUL

Start by dicing your vegetables, laying these out evenly distanced on a baking tray and cover with a sprinkling of garlic salt, smoked paprika and a crushed stock cube.

Place the tray in the oven at 180°C for 25 minutes. Check the vegetables are soft after this time by prodding them with a knife. Next, move all the ingredients into a pan and cover with hot water.

Continue boiling the vegetables until they soften completely; enough to blend them together. When ready, blend the soup contents bit by bit, seasoning with plenty of smoked paprika as you go.

Once blended, add in the cream cheese and let it dissolve into the soup. Leave for a few minutes and serve.

Recipe by Jyza Sheriff

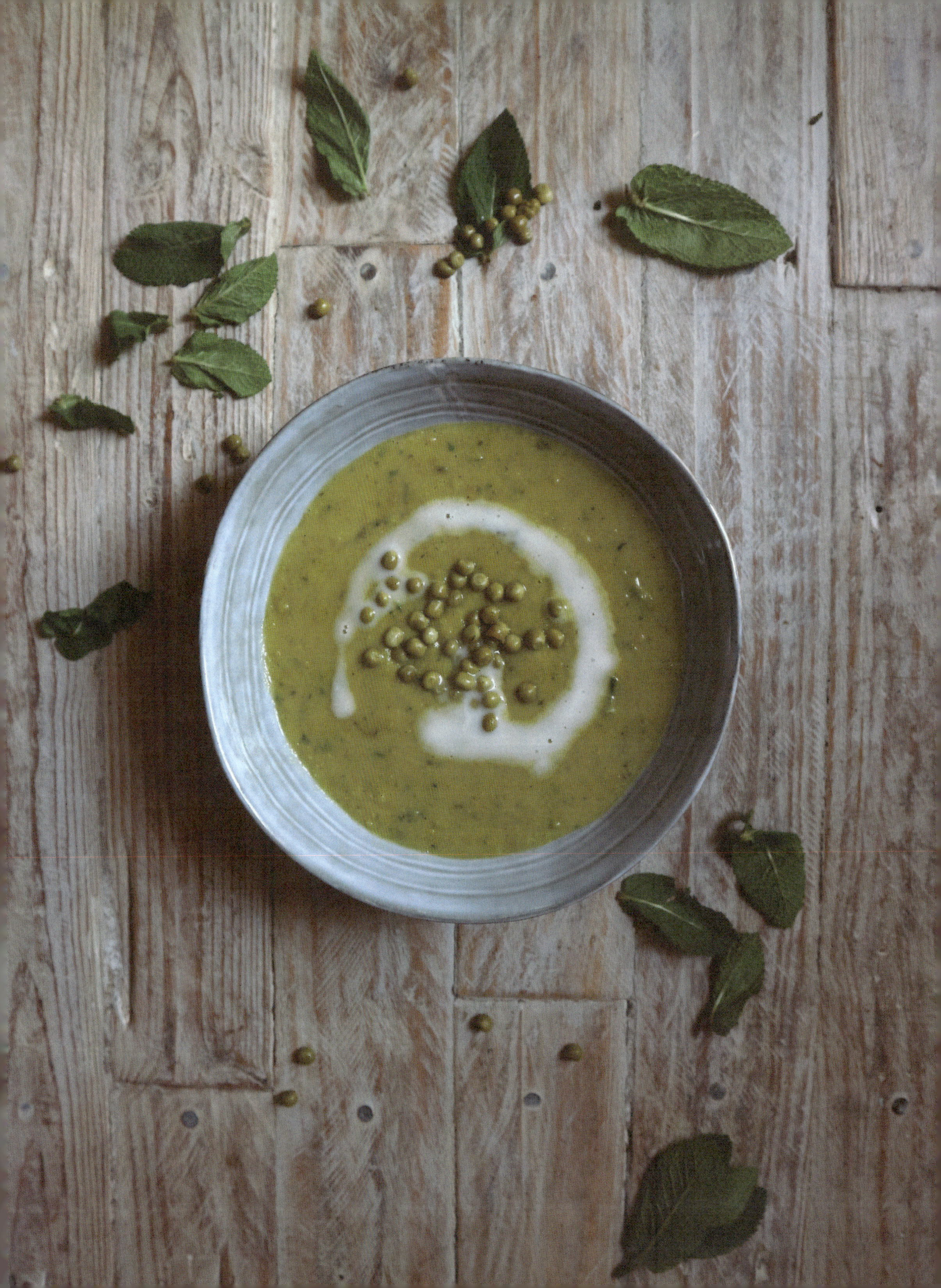

COCONUT CREAM DRIZZLE
MINT & PEA SOUP

Serves: 5 | Cooking Time: 40 Minutes

Pea soup was Mama's go-to in the winter to warm you up on those long cold days and fill you up. Although the traditional version used yellow split peas, I wanted to give this version a more vibrant tone, so I used typical green peas with a refreshing mint base so you can enjoy this anytime of the year.

INGREDIENTS

- 600g tinned peas
- 1 courgette
- 1 garlic clove
- 1ltr vegetable stock
- Mint leaves
- 2 medium potatoes
- 160ml coconut cream
- 1 tbsp vegan butter

TIME TO FEED THE SOUL

Place a large pot over a medium heat and pour in the butter. Whilst this heats up and melts, peel and crush the whole garlic and add this to the pan.

Slice the courgette and add it to the pan with the garlic. Stir the ingredients together and after a minute or so, drain the peas and tip them into the pan with the other ingredients. Add a handful of fresh, torn up mint leaves, and leave it for 8 - 10 minutes. Season this all with a pinch of salt and pepper.

Next, you will need to rinse and dice the potatoes and add it to the pot, covering all your ingredients with the vegetable stock. Leave the pot covered for 10 minutes or so until the potatoes are wonderfully soft.

Using a hand blender, blitz the ingredients together until smooth. Add two tablespoons of the coconut cream and stir the soup to combine everything.

Finally, serve the soup with some whole peas and a drizzle of the cream around the centre.

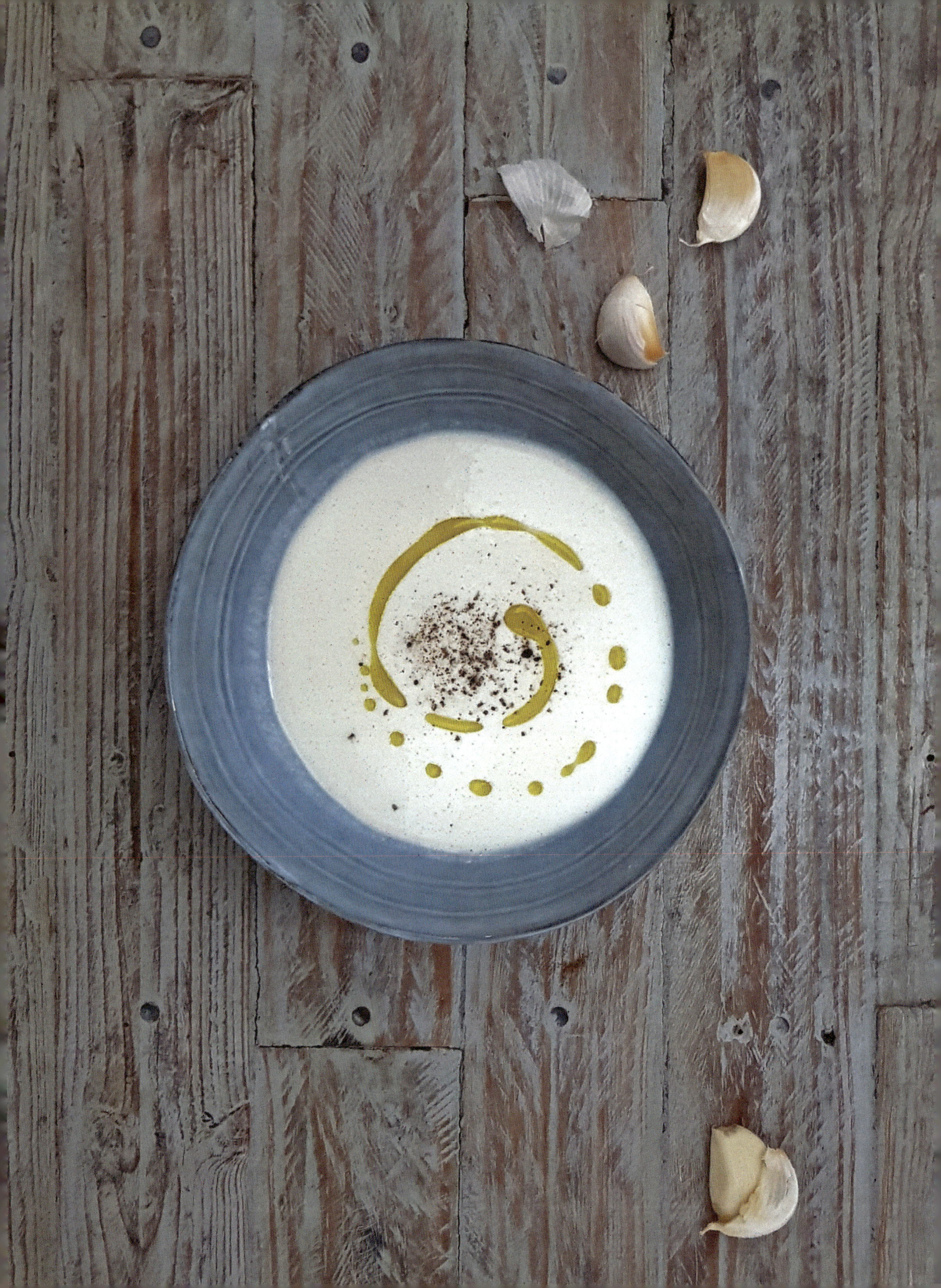

AJOBLANCO
COLD ALMOND SOUP

Serves: 5 | Cooking Time: 1 Hour

Ajoblanco is one of Spain's wonderfully light and smooth cold soups, to be enjoyed on a perfect hot summer's day.

INGREDIENTS

200g raw & peeled almonds
150g soft white bread
1 garlic clove
200ml olive oil
620ml water
Sea salt
Black pepper

TIME TO FEED THE SOUL

Soak the nuts, bread and garlic in a large bowl with the water and oil and leave it in the fridge for a few hours to completely chill. This will allow the almonds to soak up the liquid and soften.

After a couple of hours, transfer everything to a blender and blend until completely smooth. If you find yourself blending for a long time, add some crushed ice to keep the soup nice and cold.

Season with salt and pepper and serve with some almond flakes and a drizzle of olive oil.

If you want a truly traditional experience then serve this with some grapes or berries.

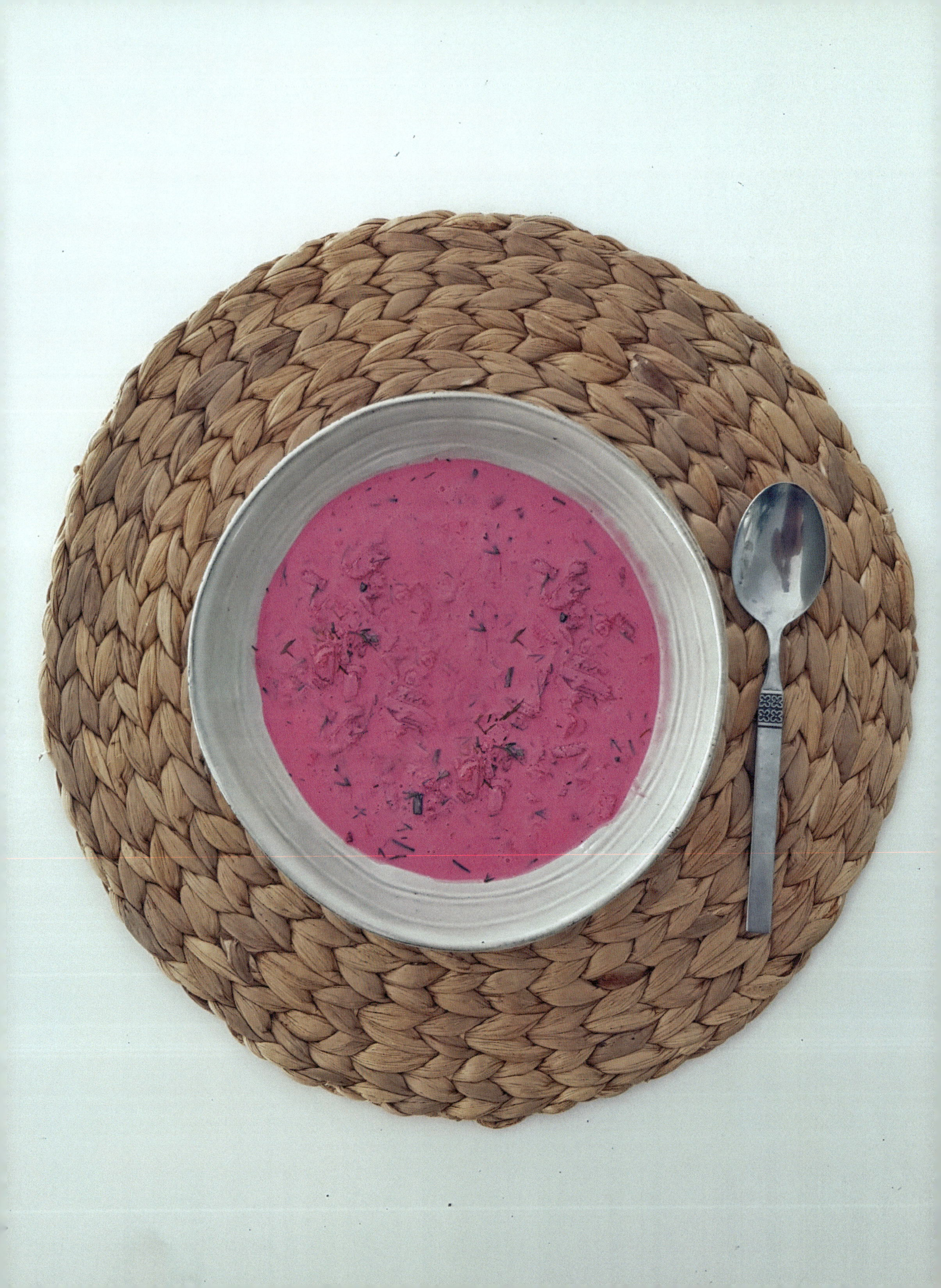

COLD BEETROOT SOUP (CHŁODNIK Z BOTWINKI)

Serves: 5 | Cooking Time: 30 Minutes

We are all familiar with Gazpacho, Spain's cold tomato soup, but have you heard of and tried Poland's alternative? This delightfully refreshing and filling cold beetroot soup is the perfect balance of sweetness, garlic, and fragrant dill, combining to form our new favourite summer dish.

INGREDIENTS

- 500ml vegetable stock
- 2 cooked beetroots
- 2 gherkins
- 2 garlic cloves
- Dill
- Chives
- 2 tsp vinegar
- 400g non-dairy cream
- 400g soy or non-dairy yogurt
- Salt
- Pepper
- 1 block smoked tofu

TIME TO FEED THE SOUL

Start off by preparing the stock. Dissolve 1 stock cube in 500ml of water, and set aside to cool.

Grate the beetroot, garlic, and peel the gherkin before grating it into a bowl with the beetroot and garlic..

Next, finely chop down the dill and chives, leaving a sprig of dill to one side for decorating.

Once the stock is cold, mix all the ingredients together, add in the cream and yogurt, and combine. Season to taste and finally add the vinegar.

Leave this in the fridge for 30 minutes to cool throughout before serving, crumbling pieces of the tofu on top.

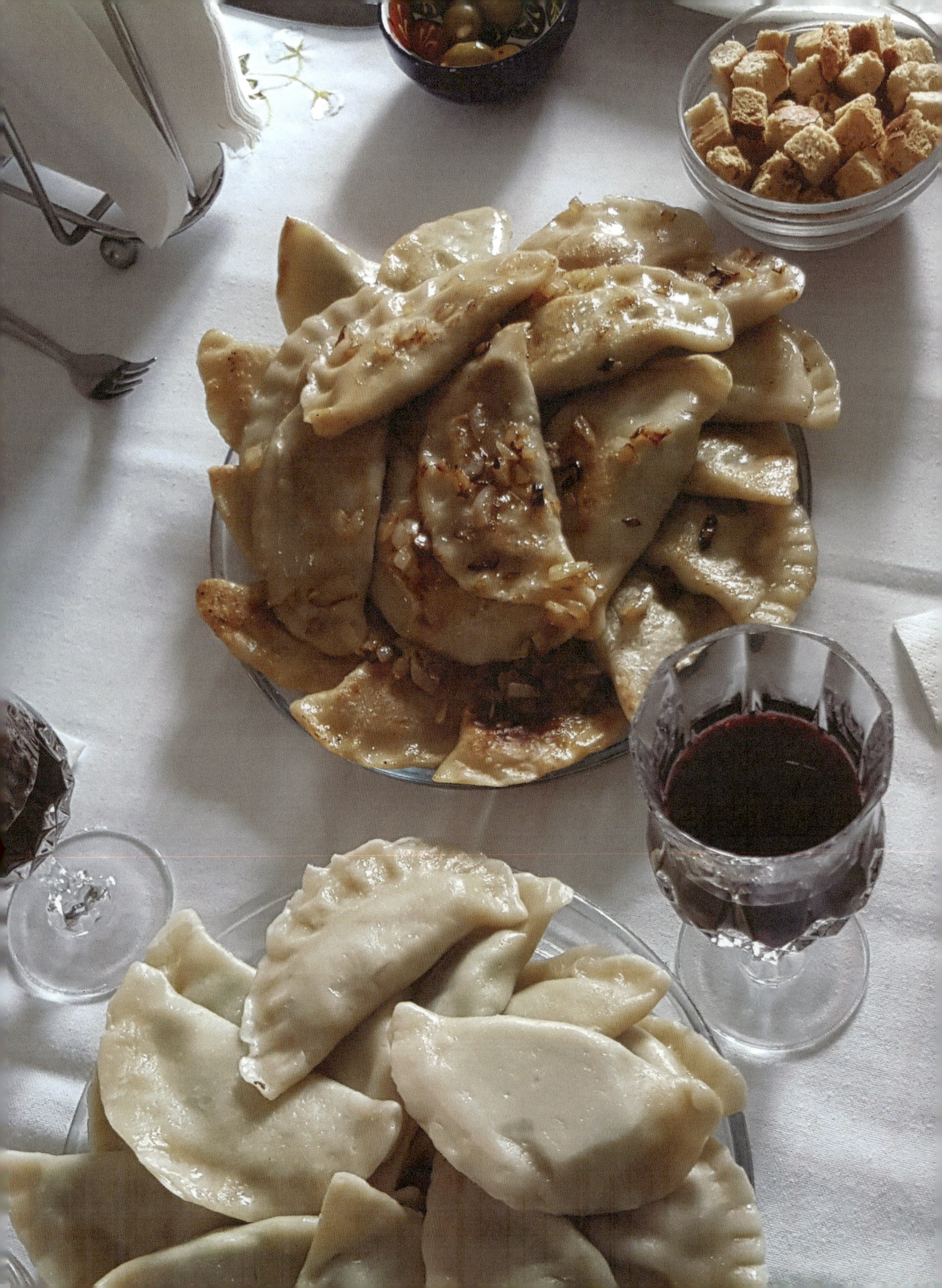

MUSHROOM & SWEET ONION PIEROGI (DUMPLINGS)

Serves: 6 | Cooking Time: 1 Hour

Discovering Polish dumplings has been a revelation! I love the fact that *pierogis* have so many variations, from savoury and soft to crunchy, creamy, and believe it or not, even sweet! WHAT?! Yep, I know, mind blown. The fantastic thing about these Eastern European treats is that once you make the dough and get the hang of shaping them all you need to do it is boil, sometimes fry and serve.

INGREDIENTS

- 480g flour
- 540g hot water
- 108ml olive oil
- 600G mushrooms
- 2 onions
- Salted butter
- Salt
- Black pepper

TIME TO FEED THE SOUL

Start by preparing the stuffing. Dice down the mushrooms into very small pieces and place them in a large frying pan over a medium heat with a dollop of butter. Do the same with the onion *(leave about a 1/4 onion's worth to one side.)* After a minute or so, dice the onions and add them to the pan with the mushrooms, stirring to combine and soften in the butter. Season with salt and black pepper.

When the filling is ready, leave it to one side and prepare the dough.

In a large bowl, combine the flour, water, and oil. Mix and knead the ingredients to form a dough until it comes away from the sides of the bowl and you can manipulate it without it sticking to your hands. Sprinkle some flour on a large worktop surface and place the dough on top.

Now roll out the dough thinly and cut into circles, *(use a bowl or something round as a stencil)*. Place a spoonful or two of the mushroom mixture in the centre and fold half the circle over. Now squeeze the ends together to seal.

Place the prepared pierogis in a bowl with boiling water and boil for a couple of minutes. Heat up a pan with a generous amount of butter and add the 1/4 onion we left to one side. Once the pierogis are boiled, scoop them out with a spoon, drain, and add them to the pan to fry on each side more a minute or so, just to crisp the outside.

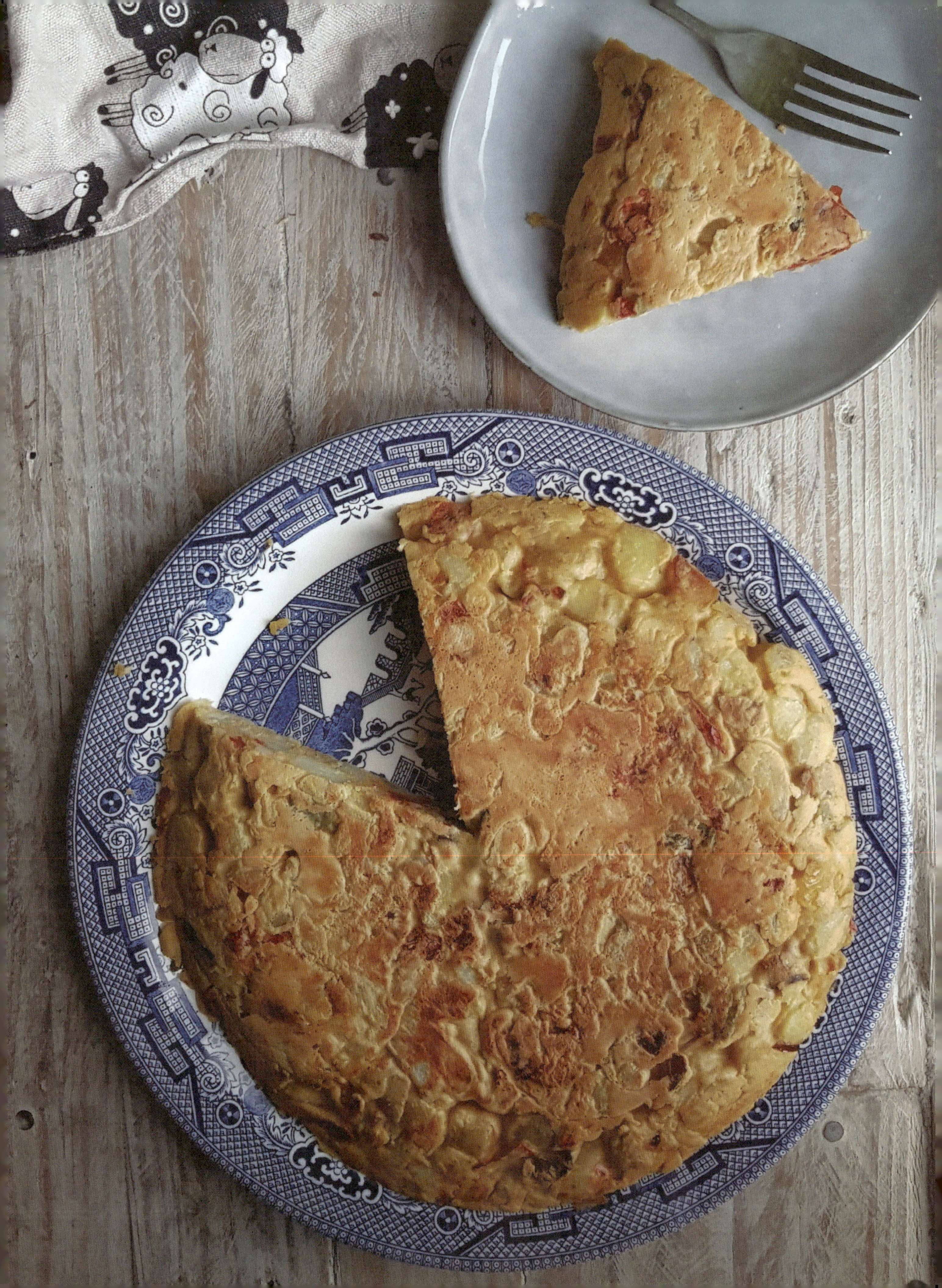

VEGAN TORTA DE PATATA

Serves: 5 | Cooking Time: 30 Minutes

What's more common around these parts than a good *torta de patata* (Spanish omelette)? It's great to take to the beach, for parties, and as a picnic snack with the family. So I challenged myself to make an egg-free version without compromising on the flavour of the original.

INGREDIENTS

- Olive oil
- 4 medium potatoes
- ½ onion
- 250g chickpea flour
- 300ml water
- Sea salt
- 1 green pepper
- 1 red pepper
- ½ tsp sweet paprika

TIME TO FEED THE SOUL

Peel your potatoes, getting rid of any black bits, and chop them into small chunks (roughly the size of dice cubes). Slice your onion and green pepper into thin strips. Season everything with salt.

Pour the olive oil into a large, deep frying pan and heat up over a medium heat. Once the oil looks hot enough *(test it by adding one potato and seeing if it sizzles right away)* add in the potatoes. Fry for about 15 minutes, until you see the potatoes soften. In a separate pan, fry the onion and peppers.

In a large bowl, combine the chickpea flour, water, and paprika, stirring until smooth. Once the chips are ready, remove the potatoes and vegetables from the pan and drain the oil. Add the vegetables to the mixture and mix thoroughly.

Pour a bit of oil into a frying pan and tip the mixture into it. Fry over a medium heat for 5 minutes on one side, then carefully flip the torta over. To do this, place a plate on top of the pan like a lid and turn the pan upside down *(so the plate is now on the bottom)*. Return the pan to the stove and slip the torta back in from the plate *(so the bottom of the torta is now the top)*. Cook for a further 5 minutes.

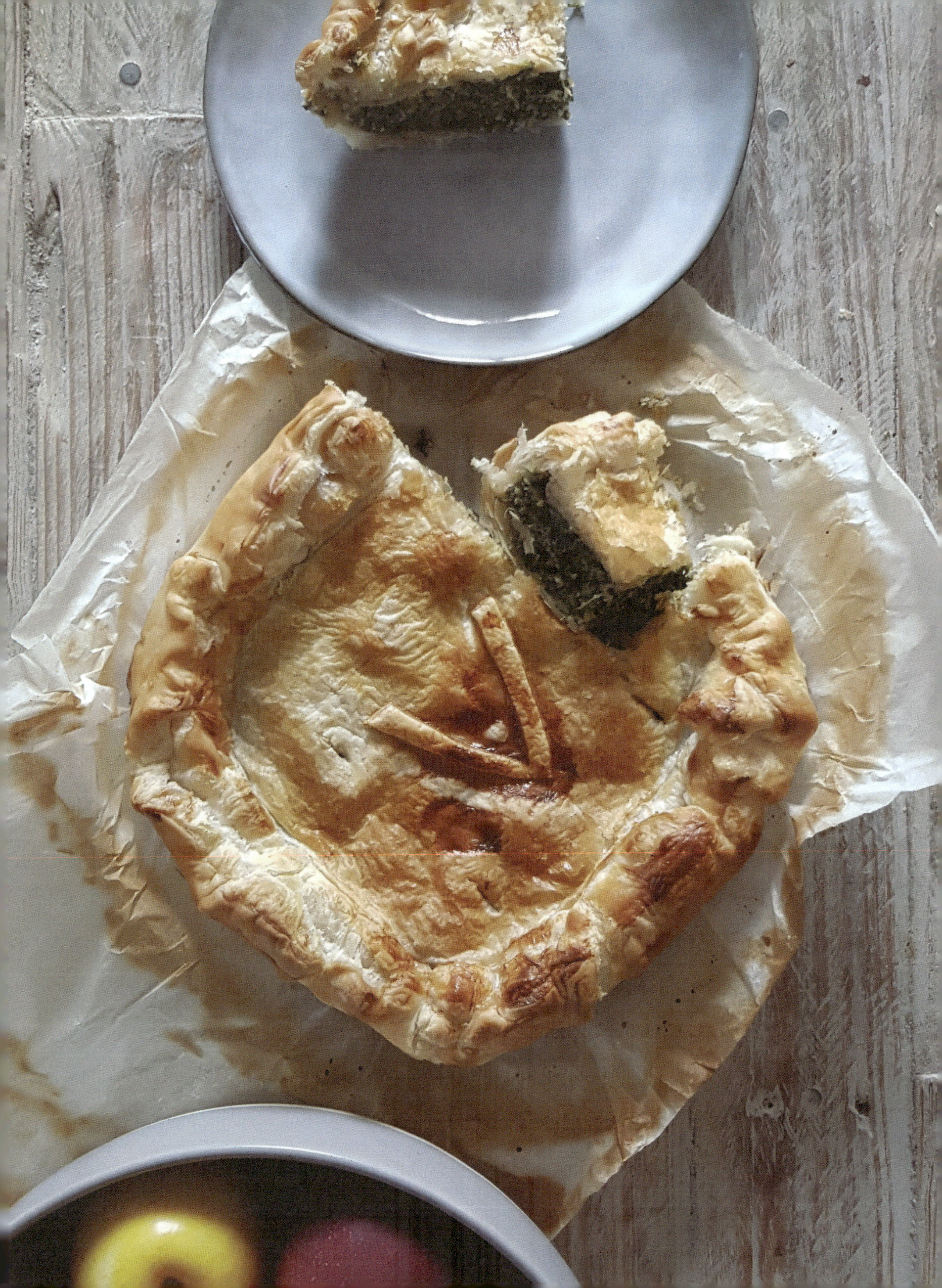

MAMA'S VEGAN TORTA DE ACELGA

Serves: 6 | Cooking Time: 30 Minutes

Torta de acelga is a must when you think of a "traditional" Gibraltar menu. Filling and nutritious, this dish has always been served up at family gatherings, so having a vegan option that everyone can enjoy was a target I'm happy to have achieved.

INGREDIENTS

Filling
- 600g fresh spinach
- 3 garlic cloves
- 150g vegan parmesan cheese
- Olive oil
- Salt
- 150g chickpea flour
- 150g water

Pie
- 500g vegan puff pastry
- 100ml nut milk

TIME TO FEED THE SOUL

Kick off this recipe by cooking and seasoning the spinach filling. One of the most important things we do for this recipe is remove the water from the spinach leaves.

Dice down and chop the garlic into little pieces and add them to a large pot with olive oil. Once the oil heats up and the garlic begins to cook, rip the spinach leaves apart with your hands and add them to the pot with a generous pinch of salt.

Stir the spinach constantly until it all reduces in size; you'll find that it releases plenty of water. Fry this for several minutes until all the water evaporates. You can squeeze the spinach with a spoon to check.

Whisk together the chickpea flour and water until smooth. When the spinach is cooked, remove it from the heat and mix it together with the grated cheese, and chickpea mix.

Next, lay out the puff pastry, Cover a medium-sized oven dish with greaseproof paper and place a layer of puff pastry in the bottom of the dish *(also covering the sides)*, fill with the spinach mix, and cover the dish with a puff pastry "lid". Brush with some nut milk and transfer the oven to bake at 180ºC - 200ºC for around 25 minutes, until the pastry is golden and puffed.

Once ready, remove from the oven and allow it to cool slightly before cutting.

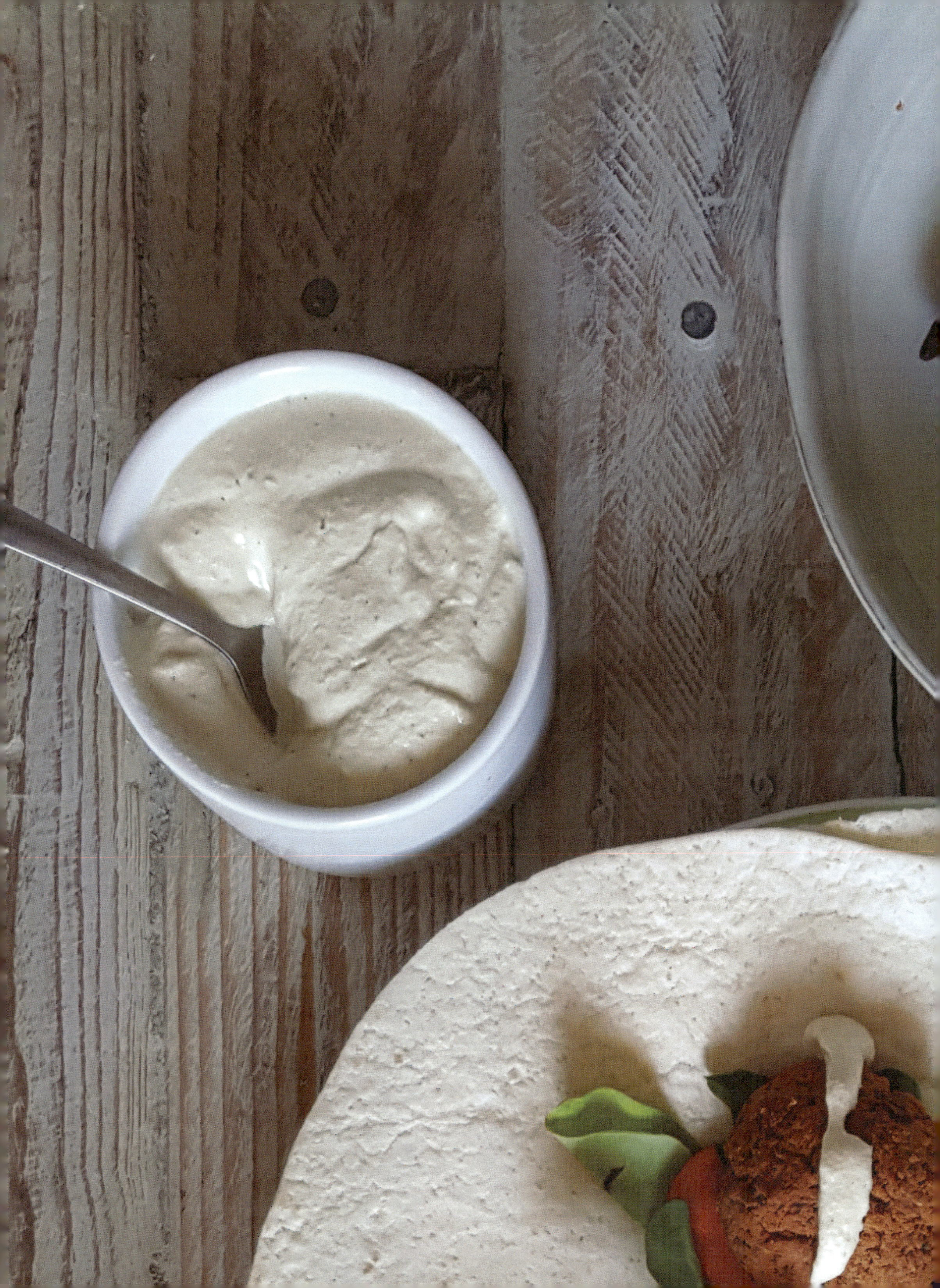

VEGAN SOUR CREAM

Serves: 4

I love how useful cashews are, as well as tasty. They can be blended to make a "cheese" sauce, but when you add some lemon juice to it, you'll have your very own dairy-free sour cream!

INGREDIENTS

- 200g cashews *(soaked)*
- 150ml water
- ½ lemon
- 1 tsp mustard
- Rock salt

TIME TO FEED THE SOUL

Soak your cashews overnight in the fridge so that they become very soft.

Place everything in a blender, including the juice of half a lemon and a pinch of salt, and blitz until everything is completely smooth and creamy.

Make sure to completely scrape all the sides of the container and blend thoroughly, then transfer to an airtight container. This will keep in the fridge for several days.

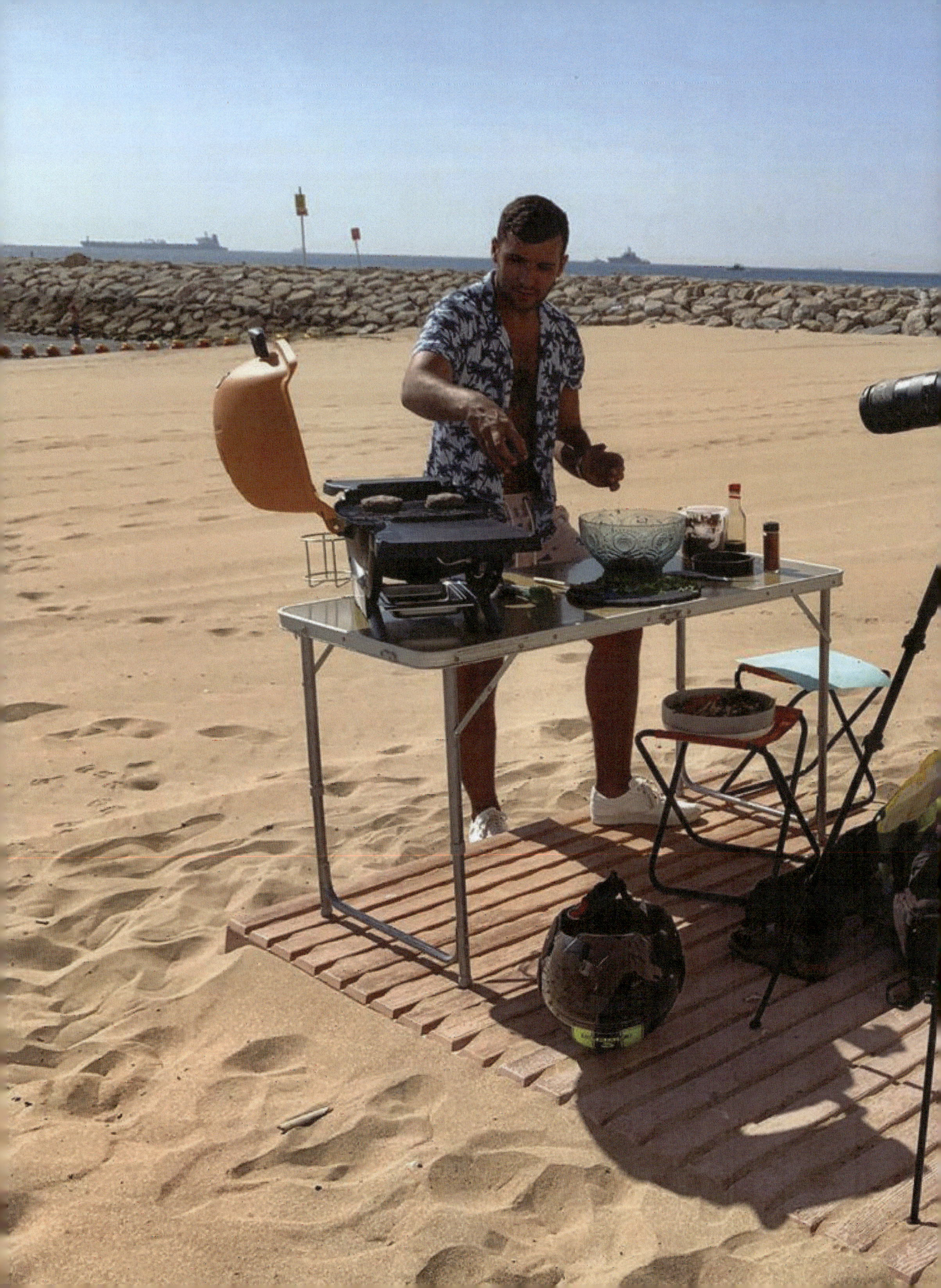

The Main Meals

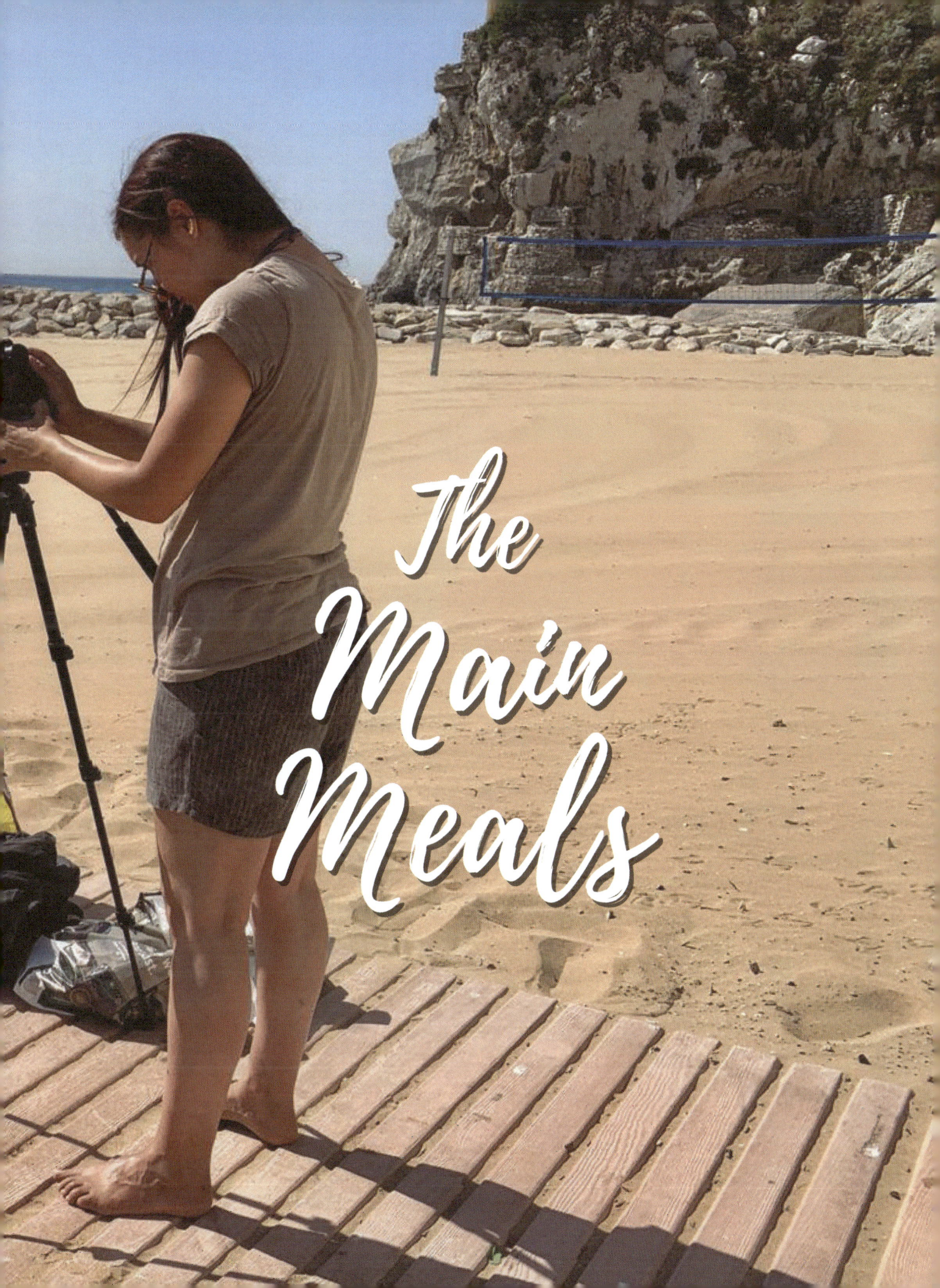

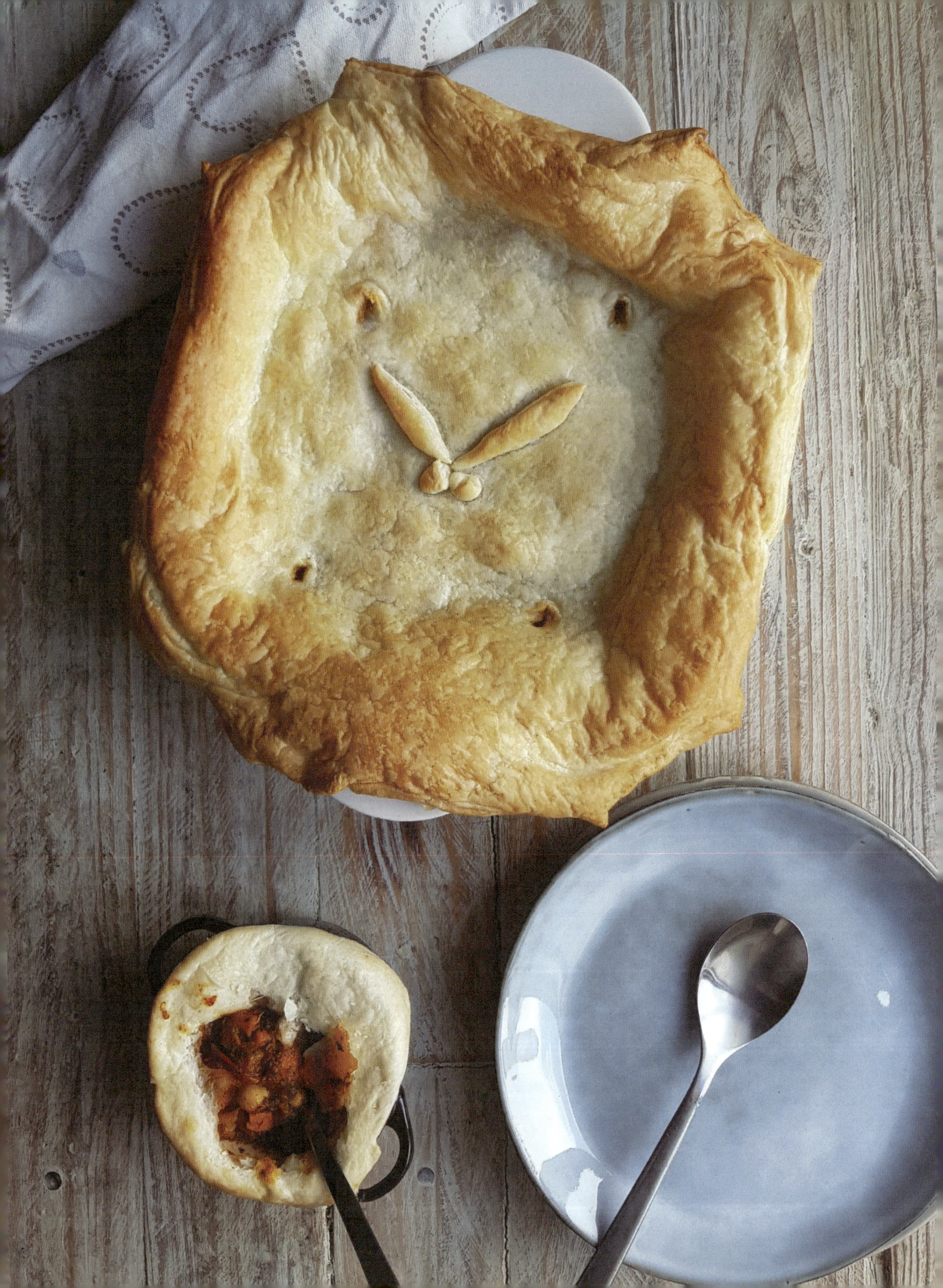

SWEET POTATO, CHICKPEA & SPINACH PIES

Serves: 4 | Cooking Time: 1 Hour

Prepare several small pies to enjoy individually, or serve up a family feast by preparing one large dish to place in the middle of the table and have everyone serve themselves. That's one way to get a conversation going.

INGREDIENTS

- 2 roasted sweet potatoes
- ½ butternut squash
- Small jar chickpeas
- Spinach or kale
- 2 fresh tomatoes
- 200g tomate triturado
- 1 fresh chilli
- 1 tbsp paprika
- Rock salt
- Black pepper
- Vegan puff pastry

TIME TO FEED THE SOUL

Peel the butternut squash and sweet potatoes and cut them down into small bite-sized chunks. Lay these out on a baking tray with a generous drizzle of oil, some crushed salt, the paprika and black pepper and ensure everything is coated evenly using your hands. Place the tray in the oven at 180°C until tender.

Once the vegetables are roasted and tender, remove them from the oven and place the tray to one side. Chop the kale, fresh tomatoes and chilli, and sauté in a frying pan. When this is soft, purée everything using a hand mixer and add in the chickpeas; stir together for a couple of minutes. Finally add in the tomate triturado.

Add the roasted vegetables to the sauce and stir in.

Line a small pie dish or individual ramekins with puff pastry and spoon the filling inside. Cover with puff pastry making sure to seal the edges and make a vent hole on top. Brush the pasty over with water or some nut milk to keep it from burning and place it in the oven at 170°C until golden and puffed.

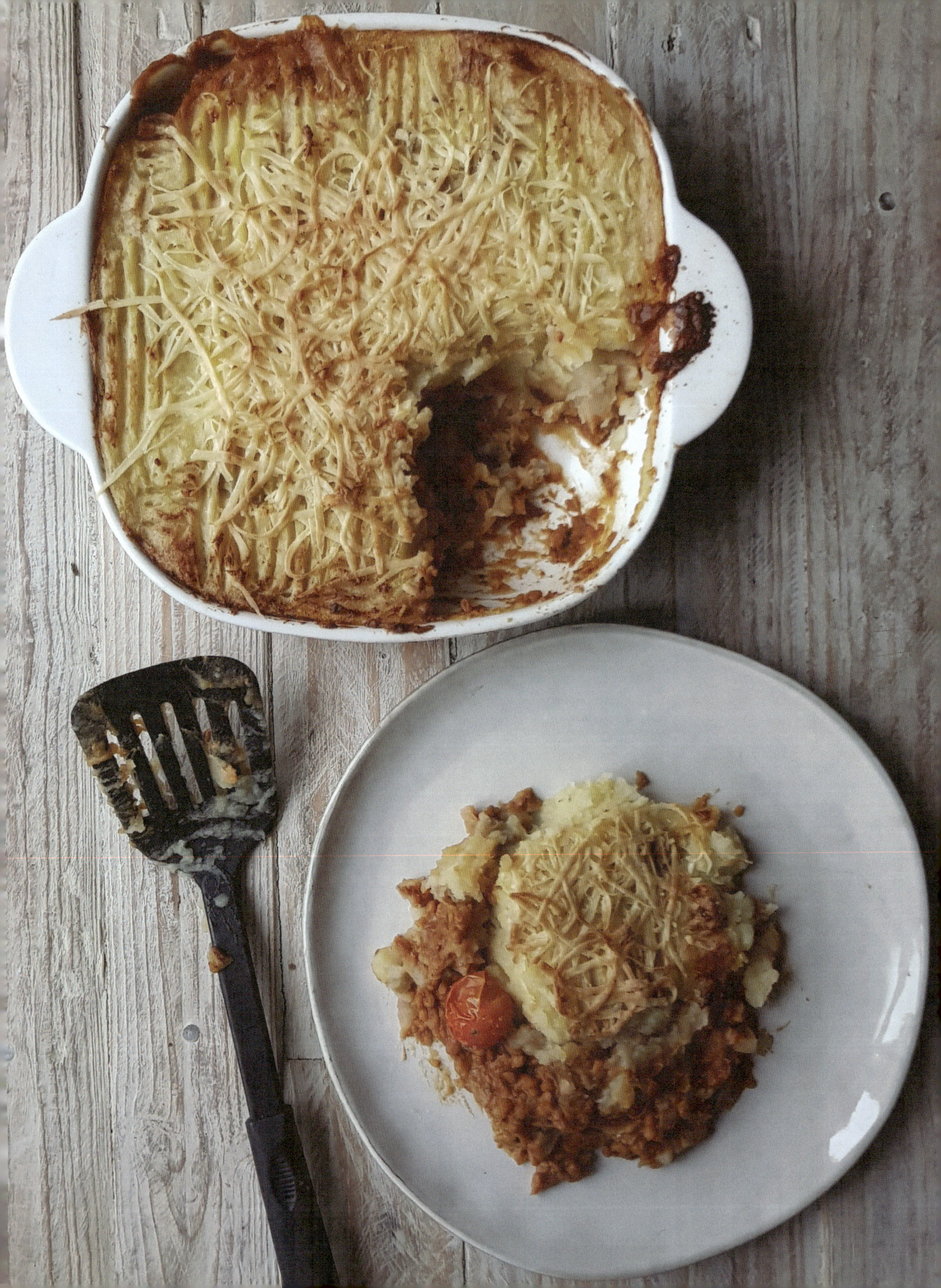

VEGAN 'COTTAGE PIE'

Serves: 5 | Cooking Time: 1 Hour

A family favourite of mine is cottage pie. Rich gravy, mashed potatoes and oh-so-irresistible melted cheese. We've swapped out the meat to give you a mouthwatering pie that you can all dig into together. Cheap and cheerful.

INGREDIENTS

- 400g jar of lentils
- 2 vegetable stock cubes
- 1 bag frozen mixed vegetables *(or any seasonal vegetables)*
- 4 large potatoes
- Vegan cheese
- Vegan butter
- 1 tsp thyme
- 1 tsp paprika
- Pepper
- Salt

TIME TO FEED THE SOUL

Preheat the oven to 180ºC

Dice the potatoes into quarters and place them in a saucepan with salt and covered in water. Leave these over a medium heat to boil until soft and tender.

Prepare the filling in a seprate pan, placing it over a medium heat and adding a dollop of vegan butter. Once melted, add the frozen vegetables. Leave these to fry while you drain and rinse the lentils.

Once the vegetables have defrosted, add the lentils, vegetable stock, thyme, paprika, and top with about 50 - 100ml of water. Stir and let it simmer until the flavours combine and the ingredients soften completely.

Once the potatoes are ready, drain them and add them back into the saucepan, add 2 tablespoons of vegan butter and mash until creamy. If you feel they need to be creamier add some more butter or even nut milk.

Now grab a medium-sized oven dish and lay out the ingredients. First the lentil and vegetable mixture and then the potatoes on top. Spread them out with a fork and cover with grated vegan cheese.

Transfer the dish to the oven and grill under a medium heat until the cheese melts and the top of the potatoes go golden and crisp.

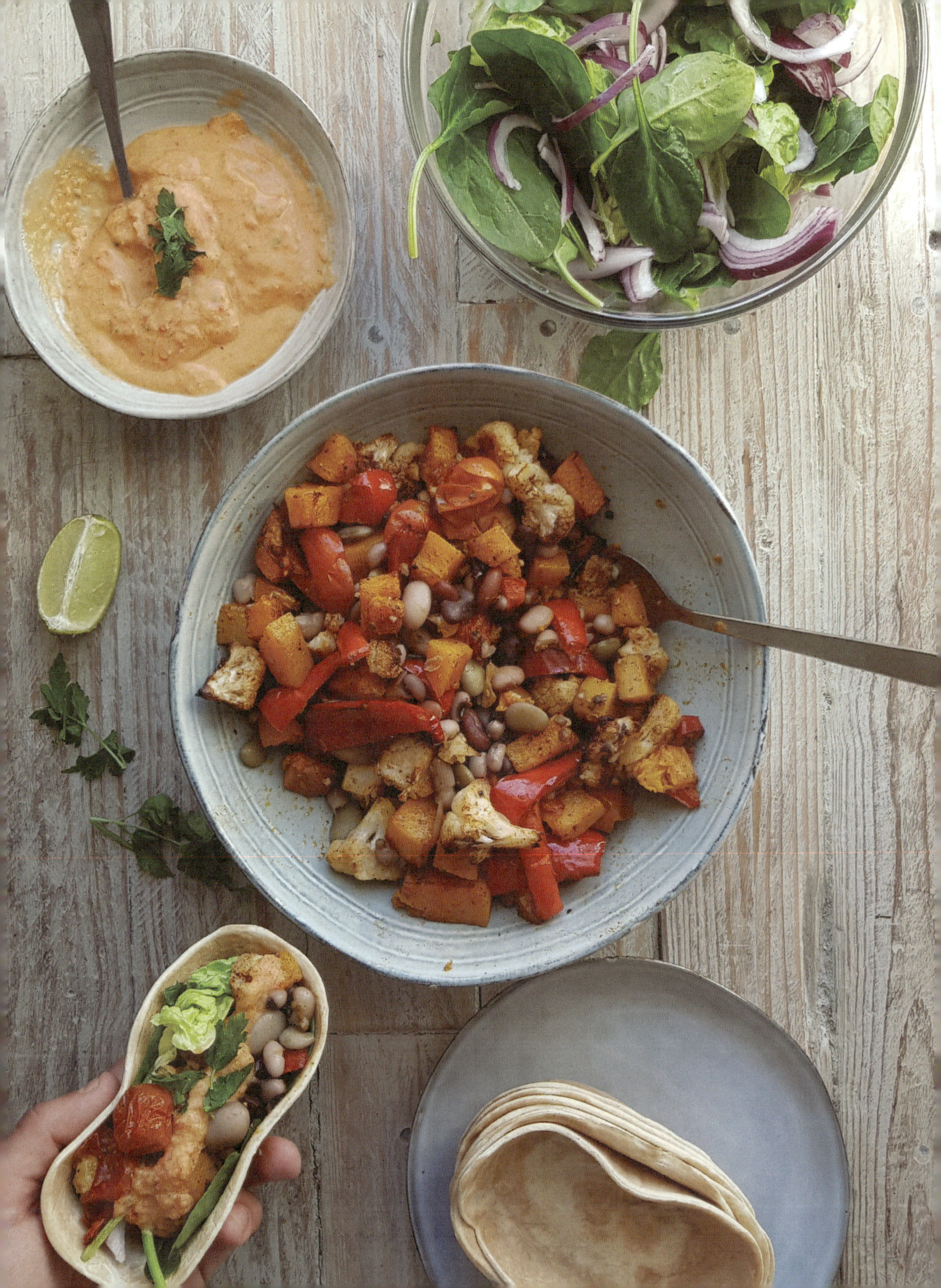

MIXED BEAN TACO

Serves: 4 | Cooking Time: 1 Hour

Tacos, burritos or fajitas, I love them all. So I created a recipe you can adapt to suit either. The butternut squash makes all the difference in this sweet vegan filling.

INGREDIENTS

- 8 large taco boats
- 1 large red onion
- 1 butternut squash
- 1 head of broccoli
- Mixed beans *(tinned)*
- 1 red bell pepper
- Spinach
- 6 cherry tomatoes
- Fresh coriander
- 1 baby lettuce
- 1 tbsp ground cumin
- 1 tbsp cinnamon
- Black pepper
- Olive oil
- Salt
- Tomato salsa
- Vegan cheese

TIME TO FEED THE SOUL

Dice the butternut squash (peeled), bell pepper and broccoli into small chunks and chuck them into a large bowl. Drizzle them with olive oil, season with salt, pepper, cumin and cinnamon and give them a good toss. Lay them out on a baking tray with the cherry tomatoes and place in the oven for 30 minutes at 200°C until soft and the edges are charred.

Whilst these are in the oven, wash your lettuce and spinach, separate the lettuce leaves and put them in a bowl. Slice the red onion and add this to the bowl too.

When the roasted vegetables are ready, take them out of the oven. Drain and rinse the beans and mix it together with the roasted vegetables, making sure to combine all the oils and flavours well.

Now it's time to stuff your tacos. First scoop the salad ingredients, such as the leaves, beans and onion into the taco, then layer it with the roasted vegetables, and finally, dress it with tomato salsa.

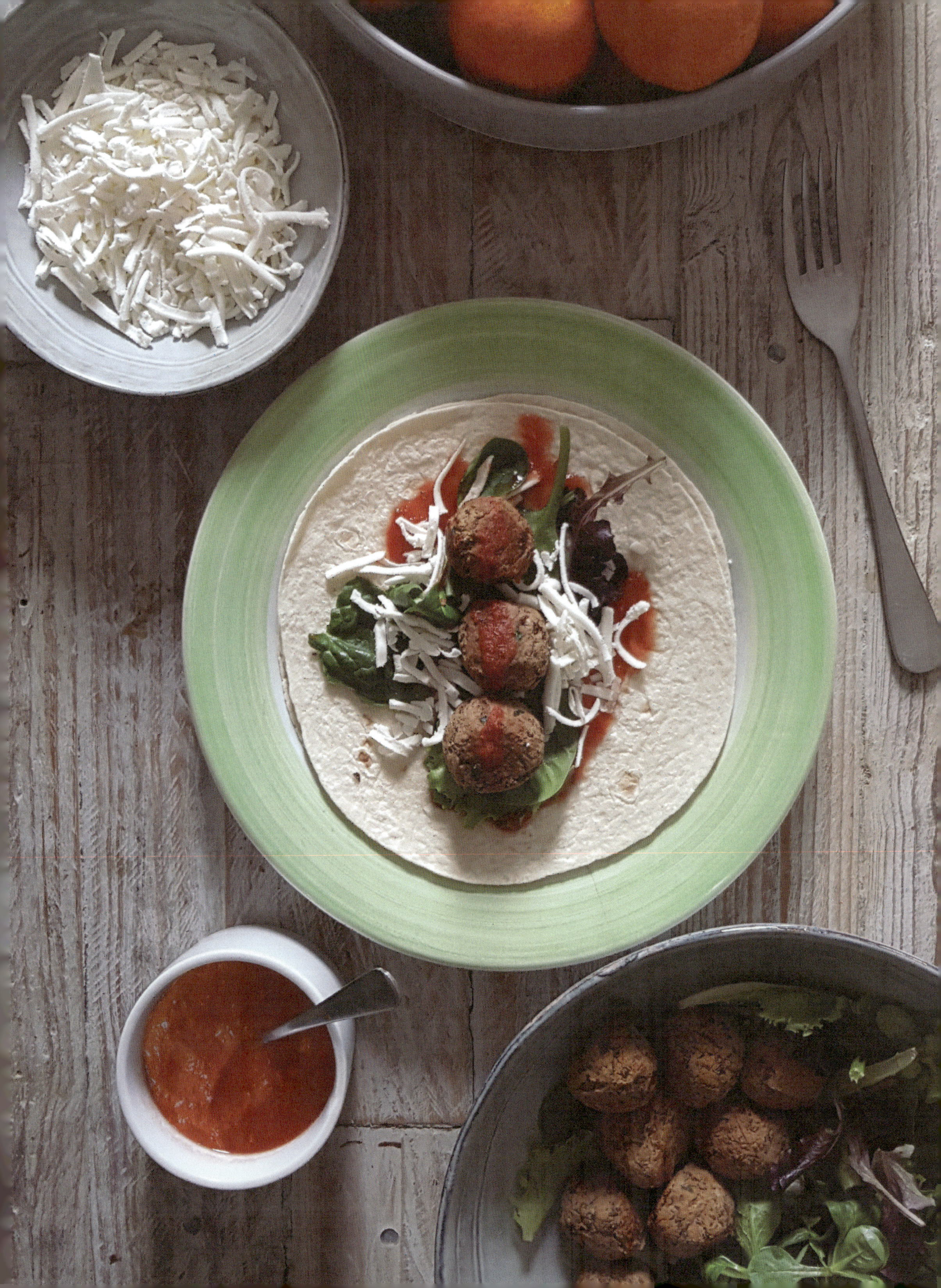

LENTIL & BLACK BEAN 'MEATBALLS'

Serves: 5 | Cooking Time: 45 Minutes

Meatloaves *(albondigas)* are a must-have in the Gibraltarian/Mediterranean diet. I've put together a fragrant and light meatball recipe that you can enjoy as a falafel wrap, or why not mix it with some tomato sauce and serve as a tapa with a glass of wine?

INGREDIENTS

1 x 400g tin of black beans
400g jar of lentils
Fresh coriander
Olive oil
4 sundried tomatoes
50g ground almonds
1 tbsp tomato puree
Smoked paprika
Pitta/wrap
Salad leaves
Vegan cheese

Sauce
1 garlic clove
1 onion
4 roasted red peppers *(pimientos asados)*
Coriander leaves
Virgin olive oil
Salt
Black pepper
½ lime (juice only)

TIME TO FEED THE SOUL

Preheat the oven to 180°C

Rinse and drain the beans and lentils and blend them together with sundried tomatoes, a splash of olive oil *(from the jar of sundried tomatoes)*, tomato puree, 1 tsp smoked paprika and coriander leaves using a food processor.

Blend until smooth and add the ground almonds.

Once blended, add to a bowl. Place a pan on a hot hob and drizzle very little oil inside, *just to lightly coat the base*, then scoop out a spoonful of the meatball mixture and roll them into balls. Lay them out inside the hot pan and gently rotate to lightly fry and crisp the ouside, ensuring they keep their shape. Transfer the sautéed meatballs to a baking tray and bake in the oven for 15 - 20 minutes until they go firm and golden on the outside.

Whilst the balls bake, prepare your sauce. Begin by peeling your onion and garlic. Place all the sauce ingredients in a blender and puree until the sauce is almost liquidised. Pour your sauce into a small dish or bowl and leave to one side.

When the 'meatballs' are ready, remove them from the oven, slice a pita bread open, place some salad leaves inside, the 'meatballs' on top and squeeze a bit of lime over the top. Finally, spoon over your homemade red pepper sauce. You can top with some vegan cheese.

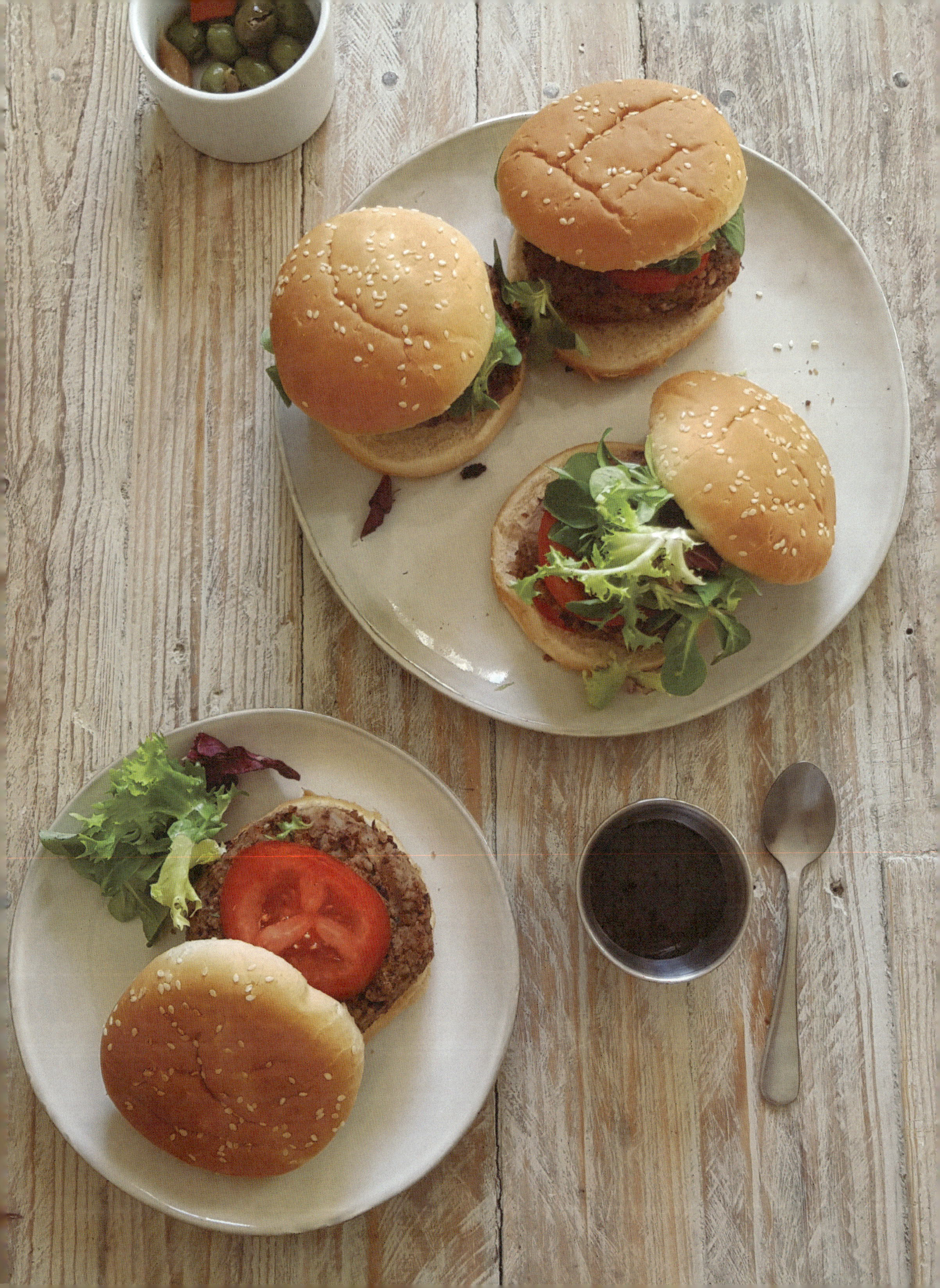

MAMA'S SUMMER BLACK BEAN BURGERS

Serves: 3 | Cooking Time: 1 Hour

A summer would not truly be complete without at least one BBQ. Who says BBQs have to be all about meat? Give these vegan burgers a go over the fire and dig in.

INGREDIENTS

- 2 tins black or red beans *(blended)*
- 2 handfuls of boiled brown rice
- 50g - 100g breadcrumbs
- ½ cooked beetroot
- Soy sauce
- Coriander leaves
- Tomatoes
- Salad leaves
- Onions
- Burger buns

TIME TO FEED THE SOUL

Blend the black beans into a paste and boil a handful or so of brown rice. Mix the two ingredients together with breadcrumbs, beetroot and soy sauce, until you have a mouldable "burger" mixture.

Shape the mixture into burger patties and place on the barbecue, or on an oiled grill pan for 10 minutes, turning every once in a while, until hot throughout and charred on the outside.

Prepare the vegetables by slicing them up, add your patties, and layer your burger buns with the remaining ingredients before serving.

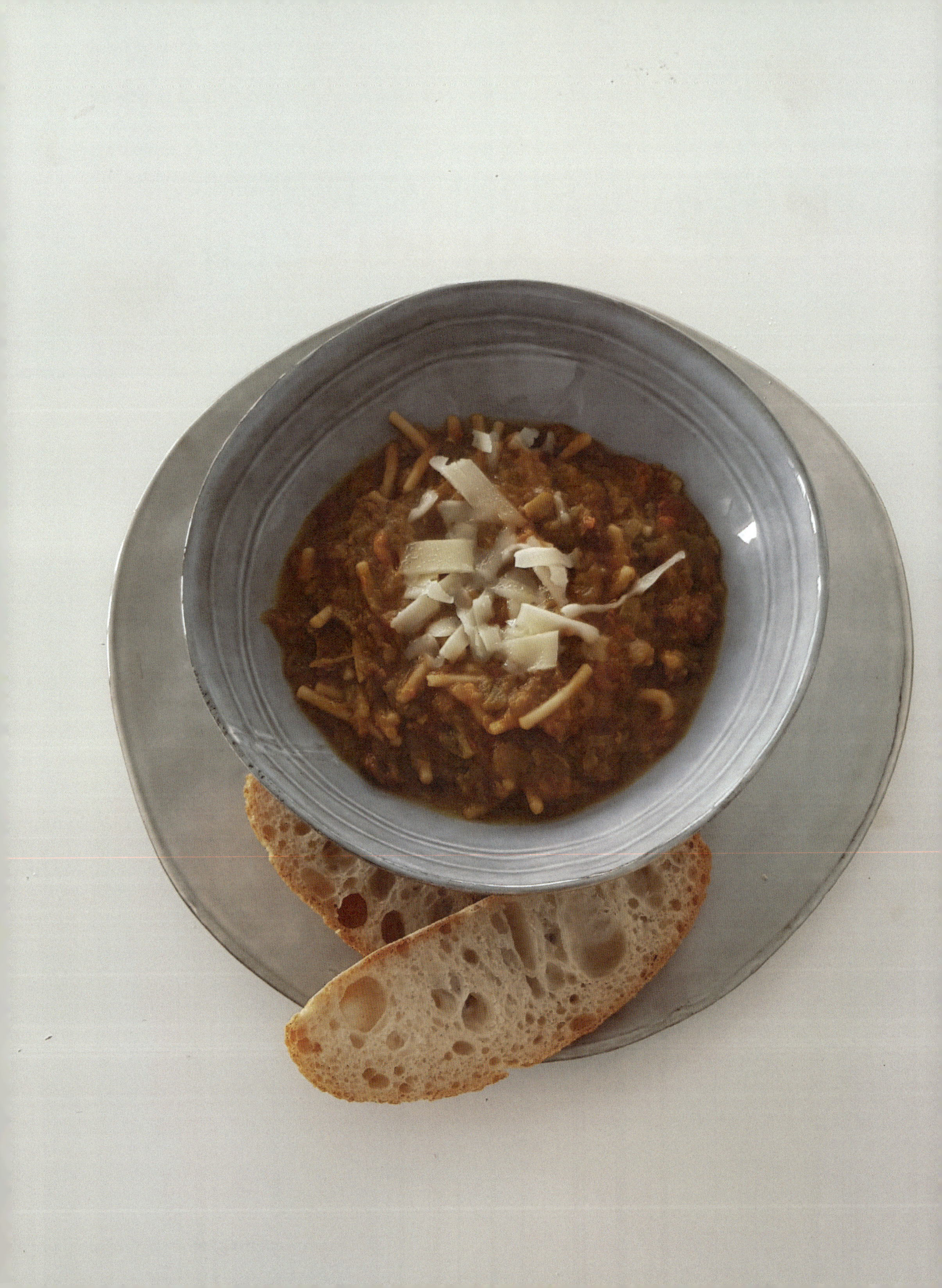

MAMA'S VEGAN MINESTRA

Serves: 5 | Cooking Time: 1 Hour

Minestra is another of Gibraltar's recipes with Italian heritage that has made its way into the hearts and traditions of Gibraltarian life. Minestra is a very typical Easter favourite, particularly on Good Friday. Served almost entirely blended or left in chunks, the wonderful part of this dish is how it varies per household.

INGREDIENTS

- 1kg runner beans
- 225g red kidney beans *(tinned)*
- 4 large carrots
- ¼ large pumpkin
- 1 large aubergine
- 2 courgettes
- 1 medium kohlrabi
- Fresh basil
- 3 garlic cloves
- Olive oil
- Spaghetti pasta *(2 handfuls, broken into smaller pieces)*
- Salt
- Pepper
- Water
- Grated vegan cheese

TIME TO FEED THE SOUL

Chop up all the vegetables, crush the garlic with the basil and salt in a pestle and mortar and place them together in a large casserole dish with a generous splash of olive oil *(all except for the red kidney beans)*. Season with salt and basil and boil with plenty of water.

Remove the vegetables from the casserole dish and blend together, then pour back into the dish and add the red kidney beans and cook for a further 5 – 8 minutes.

Add your pasta and cook until tender; this should take about 10 minutes. Allow to sit for 2 minutes before serving so the flavours mix together.

Grate some vegan cheese and sprinkle on top.

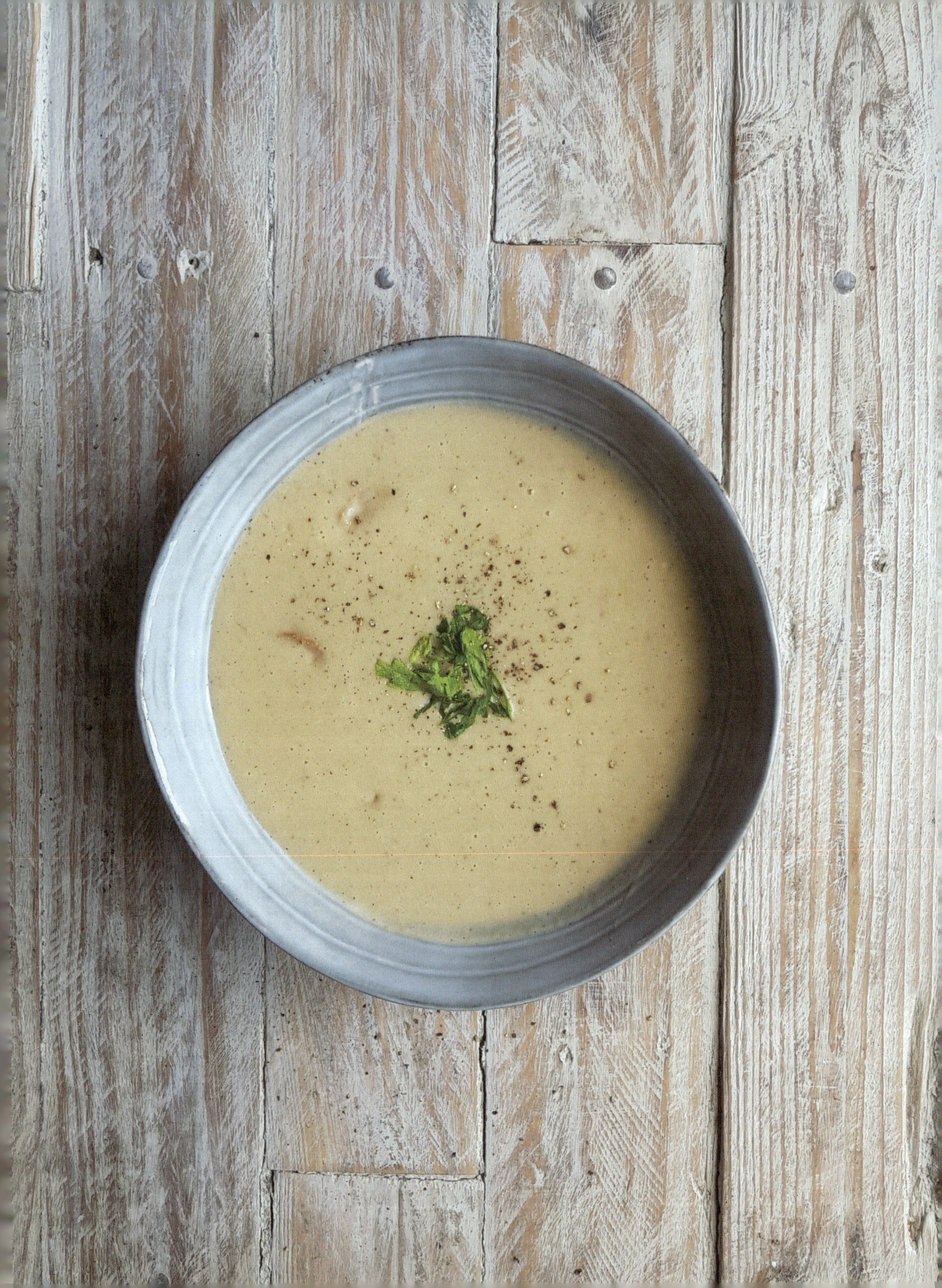

WHITE 'SAUSAGE' BROTH

Serves: 5 | Cooking Time: 30 Minutes

This recipe is inspired by the Polish dish *'Zurek'*, particularly made during Easter. Though the original recipe is thinner and uses butter, eggs and Kielbasa (sausage) all with a symbolic meaning, to make this vegan I've omitted them and substituted ingredients to make this our own blend. You could buy vegan sour cream, or if you're feeling adventurous, make your own with our recipe on p.37.

INGREDIENTS

- 450g vegan sausage
- 1.5 ltrs vegetable stock
- 2 tbsp olive oil
- 1 leek
- 1 small onion
- 3 garlic cloves
- 2 medium potatoes
- 1 tsp marjoram
- 2 bay leaves
- 250ml vegan sour cream
- 1 tbsp flour
- Salt
- Ground black pepper
- 1 tbsp chopped parsley

TIME TO FEED THE SOUL

In a large casserole dish or deep saucepan, placed over a medium heat, add oil along with chopped up leek, onion, and garlic. Cook these ingredients until soft. Add the stock, potatoes, marjoram, bay leaf and whole sausage and cook until potatoes are soft - that should take about 20 minutes.

Once everything is soft, discard the bay leaf and remove the sausage from the soup. Using a hand blender or a food processor, purée the soup.

In a separate small bowl, whisk together the flour and sour cream until smooth. Mix in a little bit of soup at a time until you have a smooth mixture, then pour the mixture into the soup. Simmer the soup, stirring constantly until thickened, about 5 - 10 minutes; season with salt and pepper to taste.

Cut the sausage into slices and add it back to the soup. Finish off by finely chopping the parsley and sprinkling it on top of the soup as you serve.

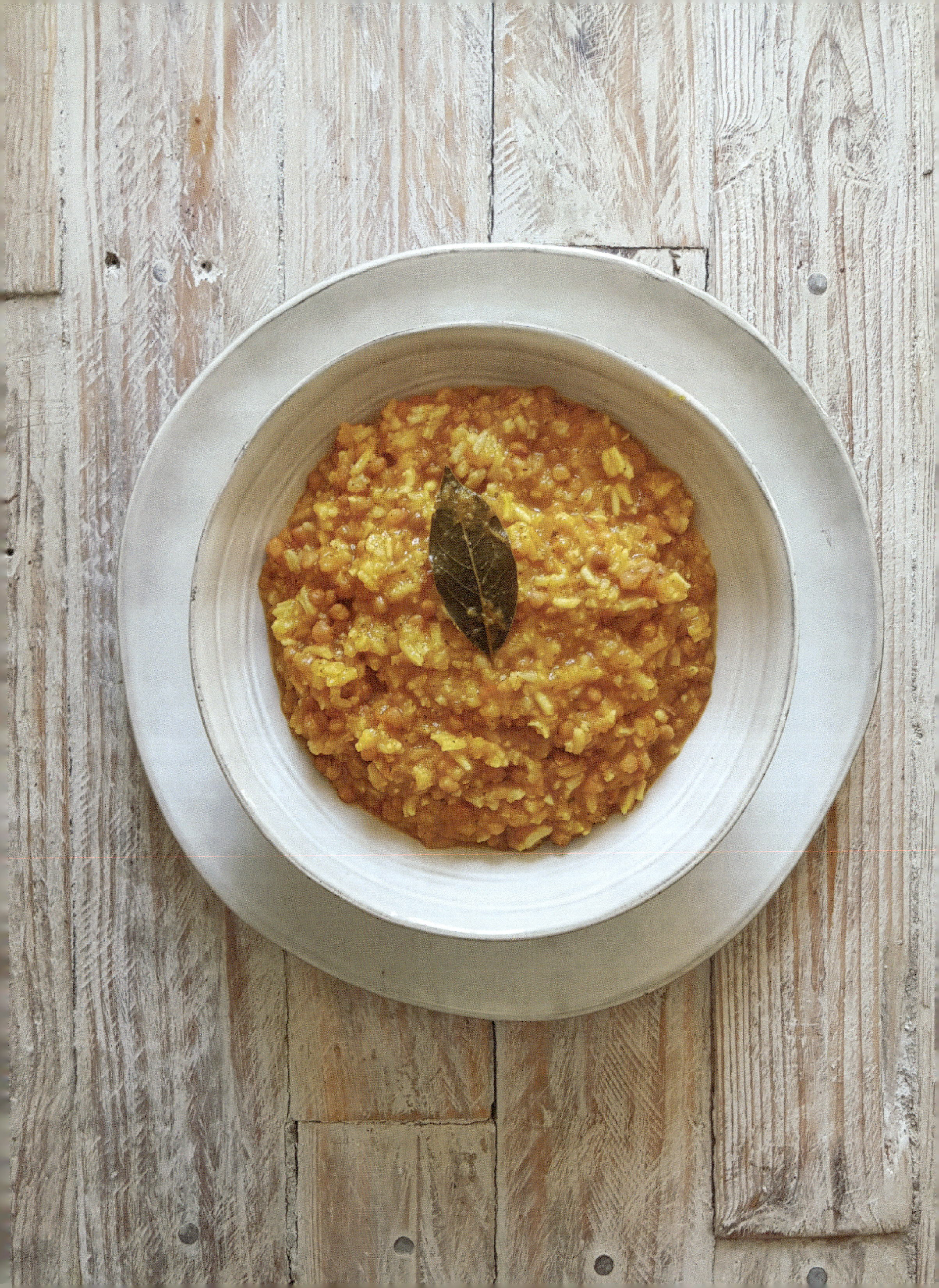

MAMA'S LENTEJAS - LENTIL STEW

Serves: 5 | Cooking Time: 1 Hour

Lentejas are a must have in any Gibraltar household. Lentils are rich in iron and protein and this traditionally Spanish inspired recipe has been one of my favourite growing up as it is jam packed with vegetables, nutrition and flavour. Typically using ingredients like chorizo and morcilla, this recipe removes the meat and brings you the same flavour using smoked paprika

INGREDIENTS

- 250g lentils
- 1 large slice pumpkin or one medium butternut squash
- 1 green pepper
- 1 tomato
- 1 onion
- 2 carrots
- 1 courgette
- 2 garlic cloves
- ½ tsp saffron
- 1 bay leaf
- Salt
- Oil
- 1 - 2 tbsp sweet smoked paprika
- 2 handfuls rice

TIME TO FEED THE SOUL

Soak the lentils in water overnight; this allows them to swell and soften. You can also used jarred lentils as an easy alternative if you're in a hurry.

Begin by placing all the vegetables and spices, except the rice and lentils, whole in a casserole dish and cover the ingredients completely with boiling water. Cook over a medium heat until tender.

Once this is all cooked, remove the vegetables and blend them with some water until thick. Add the blend back to the pot and add in the soaked lentils and rice and cook for 15 minutes or so until soft.

Allow all this to simmer together, and leave to reduce if you find the mixture too runny.

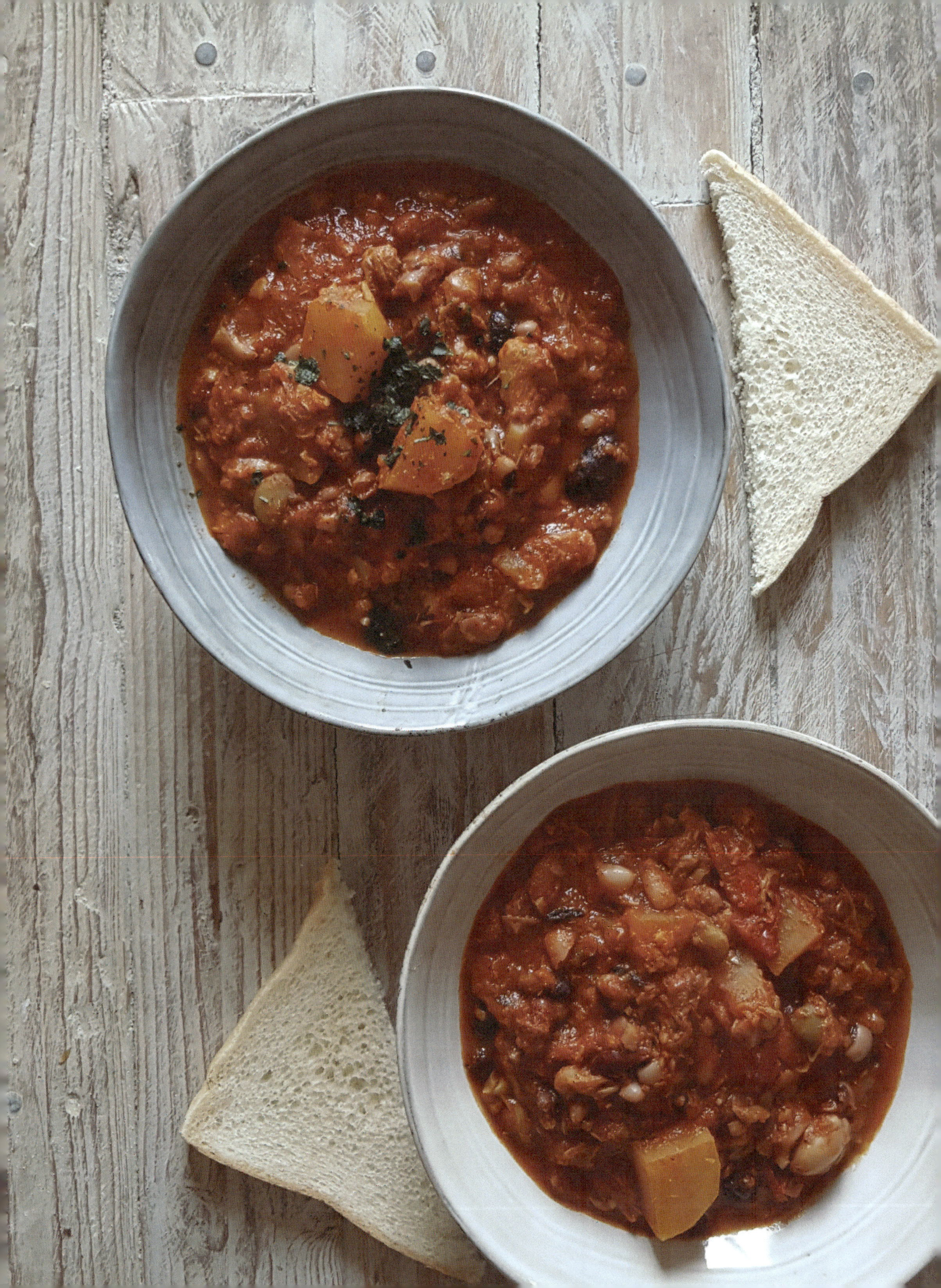

ARTICHOKE & BEAN STEW

Serves: 5 | Cooking Time: 1 Hour

I love artichokes as they have so much flavour and texture to them, but not only that, they are rich in antioxidants too. Beans are a fantastic source of protein and vitamin B so you will be ready for the day ahead with this hearty nutrient-rich meal.

INGREDIENTS

- 1 onion
- 3 garlic cloves
- 1 sweet pepper
- 400g jar artichoke hearts
- 1 potato
- 1 ½ tsp ground cumin
- 3 tsp smoked paprika
- ½ tsp ground fennel seeds
- Pinch of saffron threads
- 800g tomate triturado
- 1 jar roast peppers
- 1 tbsp fresh thyme
- 800g mixed beans
- 50g seedless Kalamata olives
- Fresh coriander
- 2 tbsp seed mix
- Olive oil
- Salt
- Black pepper

TIME TO FEED THE SOUL

Start off by slicing the sweet pepper into chunks and laying them out on a baking tray with the drained aubergine hearts. Drizzle some oil over them, a generous pinch of salt and place them under a grill on medium heat so that they char. *(Rotate them occasionally.)*

In the meantime, dice the onion and fry it gently *(on a low heat)* until almost translucent alongside the garlic. You can keep the garlic whole for this one.

Once the onion and garlic are soft, peel the garlic *(or squeeze them out of the skin)* and pop them into a blender with 3 roasted peppers from the jar. Pour the tomate triturado into the blender and blend until smooth, adding the herbs and spices *(except the saffron)*.

By now the vegetables under the grill should be nice and tender and wonderfully charred. Take them out of the grill place them in a deep pan, pour the sauce we blended together on top and add in the beans and olives, and 1 diced up potato,

Pour about 50ml of water into the pot, the pinch of saffron threads, a sprinkle of salt and pepper and allow the ingredients to simmer together, making sure to stir occasionally until the potato is soft.

Finally, once you see the sauce is reducing and that the flavours have combined, serve this by sprinkling the seed mix on top and chopping up some fresh coriander to garnish.

You can serve this as-is or alongside some rice, couscous or simply some crusty bread.

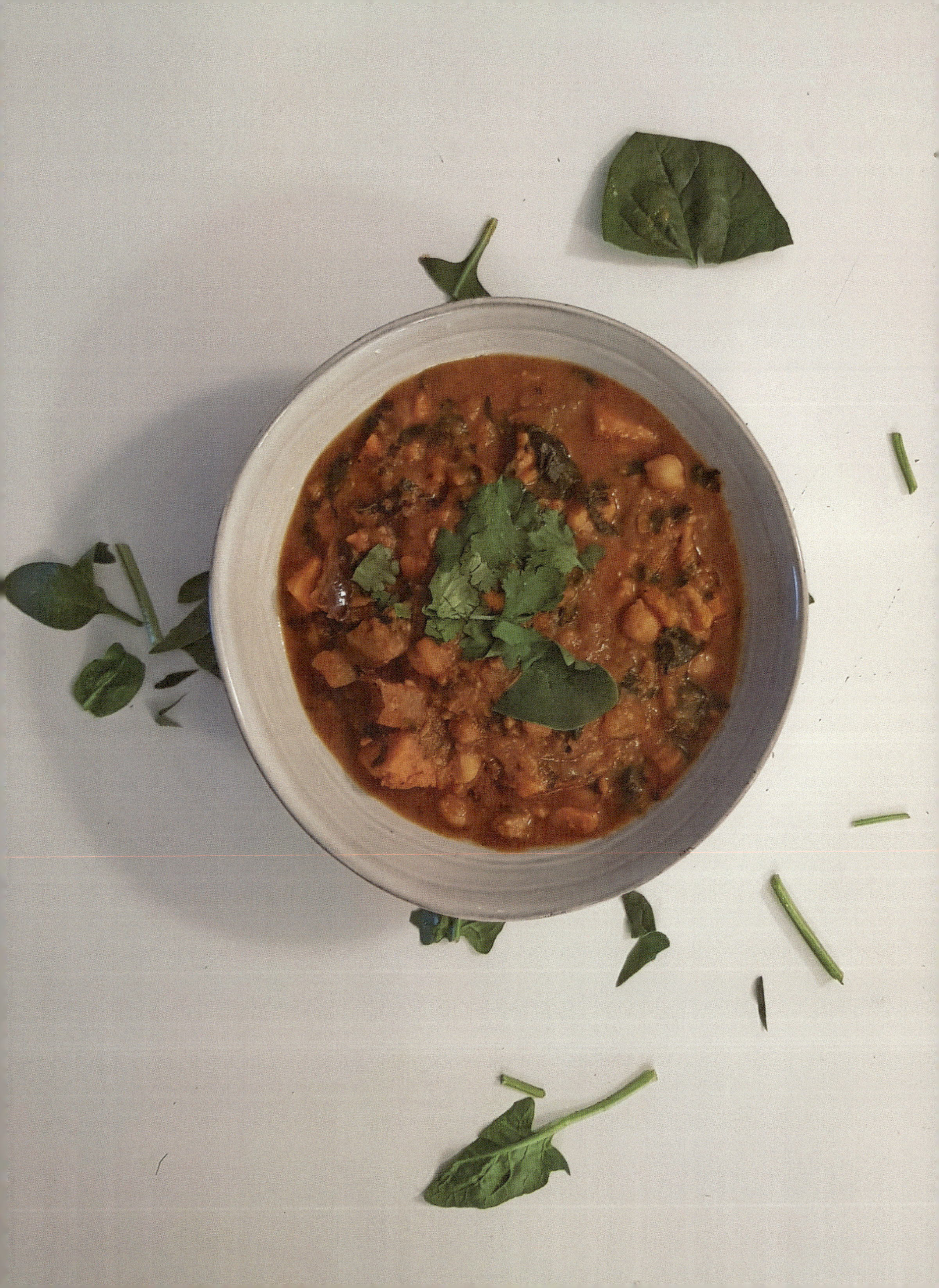

SWEET POTATO, CHICKPEA & SPINACH COCONUT CURRY

Serves: 5 | Cooking Time: 1 Hour

How hot do you like your curry? This sweet-based curry can be adapted to suit all hotness levels. If you want it with a real kick then add some spicy paprika or chillies into the mix.

INGREDIENTS

- 1 scoop coconut oil
- 1 small onion
- 1 aubergine
- 3 garlic cloves
- Fresh ginger
- 3 tbsp tomato puree
- 2 tsp ground cumin
- 3 tsp curry powder
- 2 tsp garam masala
- 150g coconut cream
- 400g tin tomate triturado
- 1 litre water
- 2 large sweet potatoes
- 400g jar of chickpeas
- 1 packet spinach
- Fresh coriander

TIME TO FEED THE SOUL

Melt a scoop of coconut oil in a large pan over a medium heat. Finely chop down the garlic and onion and fry in the coconut oil. Whilst they are frying, peel the outer skin of the ginger and shred the ginger into the pan.

Peel and chop down the sweet potatoes into cubes. Drain the chickpeas out of the jar and rinse them. Once the onion are garlic are soft and tender add in the sweet potatoes and chickpeas.

Add the spices to the pot along with the other ingredients. Stir everything together and leave it to stew until the sweet potatoes are tender. This should take around 20 - 30 minutes. Make sure to stir occasionally and top up with water if required.

Boil some rice or quinoa and serve with some shredded coriander sprinkled on top.

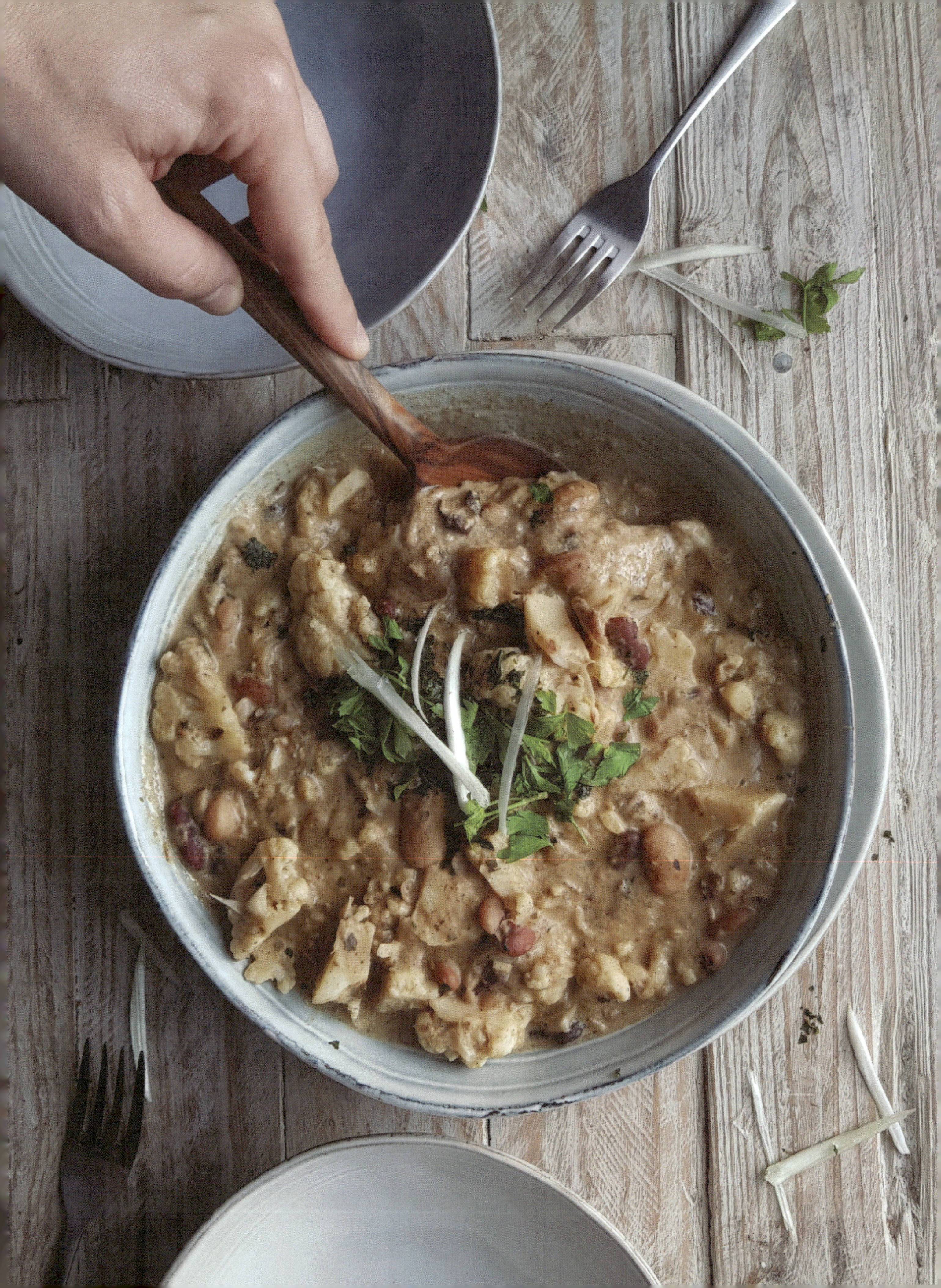

BEAN & CAULIFLOWER GREEN CURRY

Serves: 4 | Cooking Time: 45 Minutes

Try this fragrant Thai dish, rich in coconut, peppers, fragrant lemongrass and ginger, this dish is inviting and warming. Add some great textures and flavour to your dish with the cauliflower and protein-rich beans.

INGREDIENTS

- Sesame seed oil
- 1 spring onion
- 2 garlic cloves
- 4 tbsp green or red Thai curry paste* *(vegan-friendly)*
- 400ml coconut cream
- 1 large cauliflower
- Soy sauce
- 1 medium broccoli
- 200g tin mixed beans
- Small ginger root
- Fresh coriander
- ½ lime
- 200ml water

*Check the ingredients carefully as some contain fish oil as part of the mixture.

TIME TO FEED THE SOUL

Slice the garlic and spring onion into thin strips and fry in a generous splash of oil over a medium heat. Whilst the two ingredients are frying, shave and discard the outside skin of the ginger and grate the rest into the pan.

Once you see the onion softening, add curry paste to the pan and stir in so as to combine and merge the aromatic flavours together.

After a couple of minutes, making sure not to burn the garlic and onion, pour in the coconut milk and a drizzle of soy sauce. Cut a lime in half and squeeze into the pot.

Rinse the cauliflower and broccoli and dice into chunks; quickly fry this separately over a high heat to char the outside and add to the pot.

Drain your tin of soaked beans, rinse and add this to the pot too. Leave everything to stew for 5 - 10 minutes until the cauliflower and broccoli soften.

Finish by tearing fresh coriander and tossing it into the pot. Let it sit for a minute and serve.

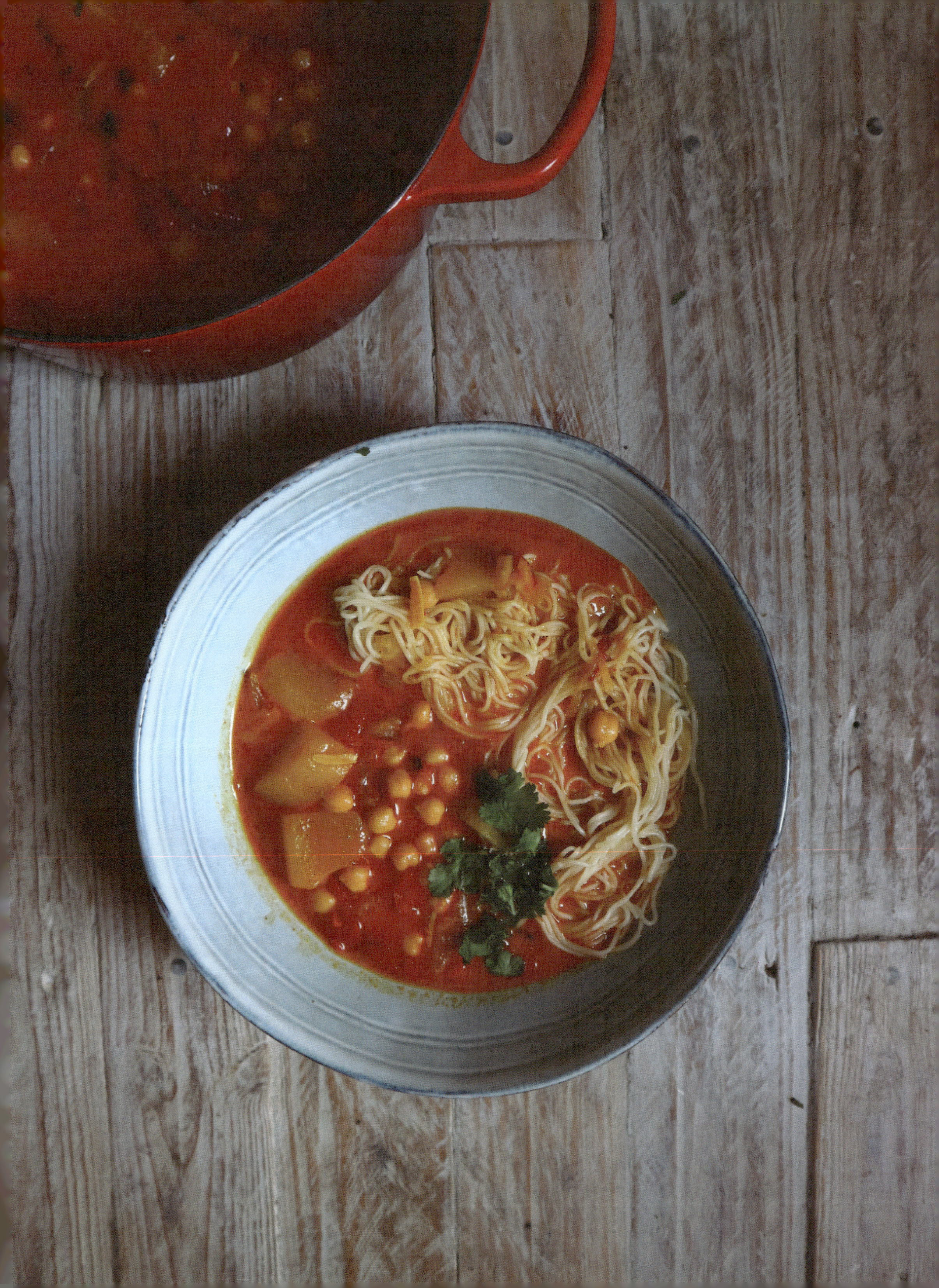

YELLOW MANGO CURRY

SERVES: 3 | COOKING TIME: 30 MINUTES

If you're a fan of Thai food and oriental flavours with a savoury-sweet vibe then this recipe is for you. Each ingredient blends together beautifully to provide you with natural sweetness from the mango, peppers and onions, whilst the coconut, ginger and red curry paste provide a burst of earthy and fragrant flavours.

INGREDIENTS

- 2 soft ripe mangoes
- 1 red bell pepper
- 1 red onion
- 200g soaked chickpeas
- 2 tbsp coconut oil
- 2 garlic cloves
- 1 red chilli *(optional)*
- 400ml coconut milk
- 160ml coconut cream
- 1 tsp turmeric
- Fresh ginger
- Soy sauce
- Fresh coriander *(optional)*
- 125g udon noodles
- Red curry paste *(with no fish)*

TIME TO FEED THE SOUL

Slice the onion, garlic and peppers into thin strips. In a large casserole dish place 2 tablespoons of the coconut oil, leaving it to melt. Once the oil has melted, add the sliced vegetables and grated ginger to the dish.

After a couple of minutes the vegetables should be softer; add in three tablespoons of the red curry paste, stir in with the vegetables, then add the coconut milk, coconut cream, teaspoon of turmeric and a tablespoon of soy sauce. Allow the ingredients to simmer together and combine.

Once the ingredients in the casserole dish are simmering and bubbling add in the chickpeas. *(I add them at this point in the recipe as the soaked chickpeas are already soft.)*

After a couple of minutes, peel and dice your mango into small chunks. Now it's time to include this in the curry mixture and lower the heat. Stir the ingredients, break some coriander over your dish, and cover the pot, leaving it to sit for a few minutes whilst you boil the noodles.

In a clean pot boil some water with a pinch of salt and add the noodles, until they soften. To serve you could either mix the noodles in with the curry or drain and serve the noodles in individual bowls and pour the curry sauce over the top.

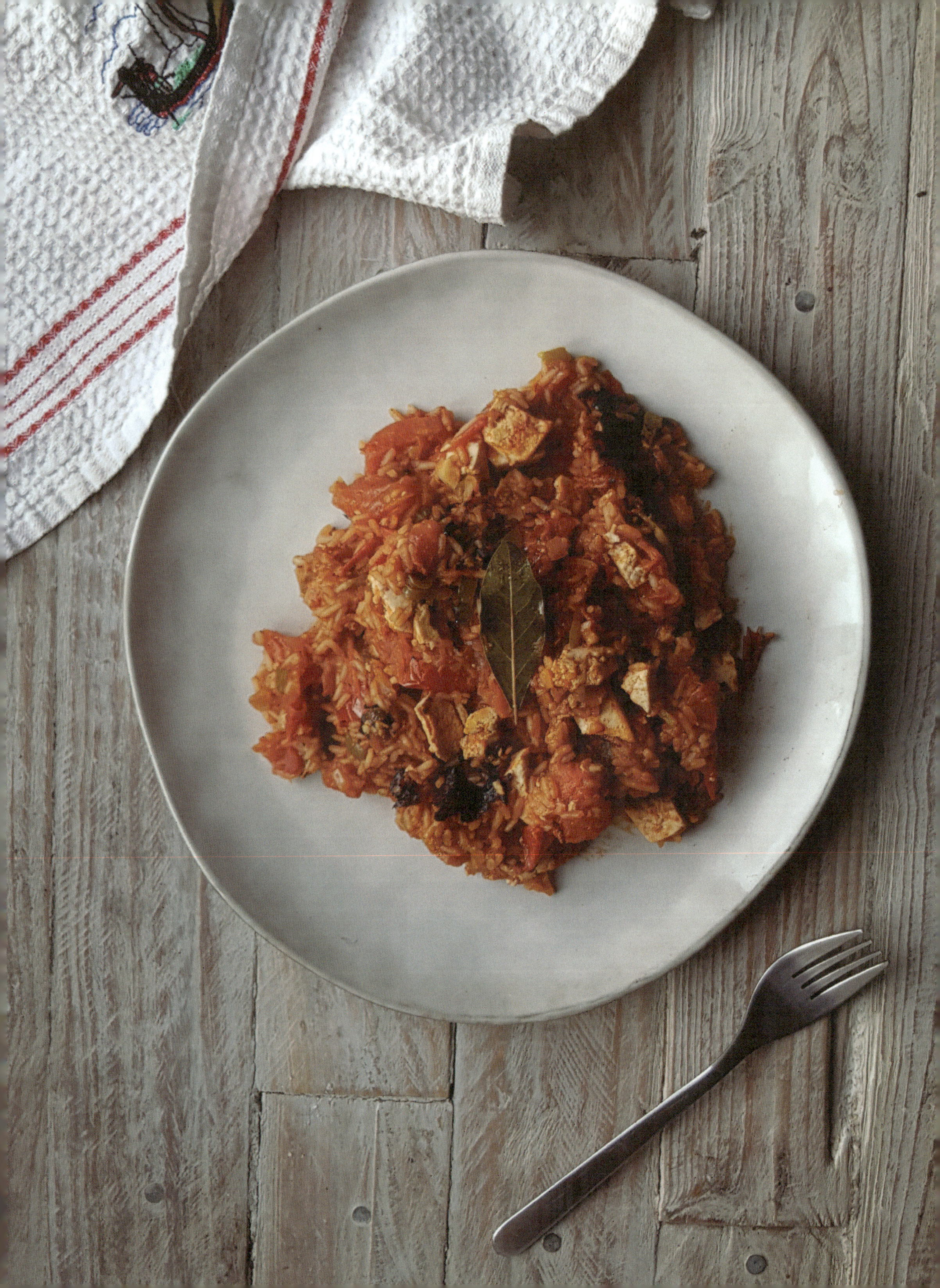

MAMA'S VEGAN PAELLA

Serves: 5 | Cooking Time: 1 Hour

Paella is a Spanish classic and a favourite of many in Gibraltar. Usually consisting of meat or fish, this traditional dish can now be adapted using tofu so that you can enjoy it in almost the same way, including the delicious socarrat *(the delicious, crispy bottom layer)*.

INGREDIENTS

- 6-8 tomatoes
- 1 large onion
- 2 long frying peppers
- 3 garlic cloves
- Saffron *(pinch)*
- 280g extra firm tofu
- Olive oil
- 100g petits pois *(small peas)*
- Salt
- Bay leaf
- 2 tbsp tomato puree
- 1 cube vegetable stock
- 200g paella rice

TIME TO FEED THE SOUL

Place a pan over a low to medium heat with a splash of olive oil and begin by making a refrito. Do this by finely dicing your onion and garlic and frying until translucent, then dicing your peppers and adding them to the pan along with your onions and garlic. Cook until soft.

Once soft, chop your tomatoes and add to the pan. Continue to gently fry until the tomato turns soft and begins to puree a little.

Dice tofu into chunks and add to the pan with the vegetables and saute in the tomato refrito. After a minute or two, add the rest of the ingredients and top up with water, covering all your ingredients.

Give the pan one good stir then cover and leave to simmer on a low to medium heat until the rice is ready. The rice should be soft with a very little bite.

Remove the lid and keep on a low heat for an extra minute or two. This will remove excess moisture and leave a perfect paella to enjoy.

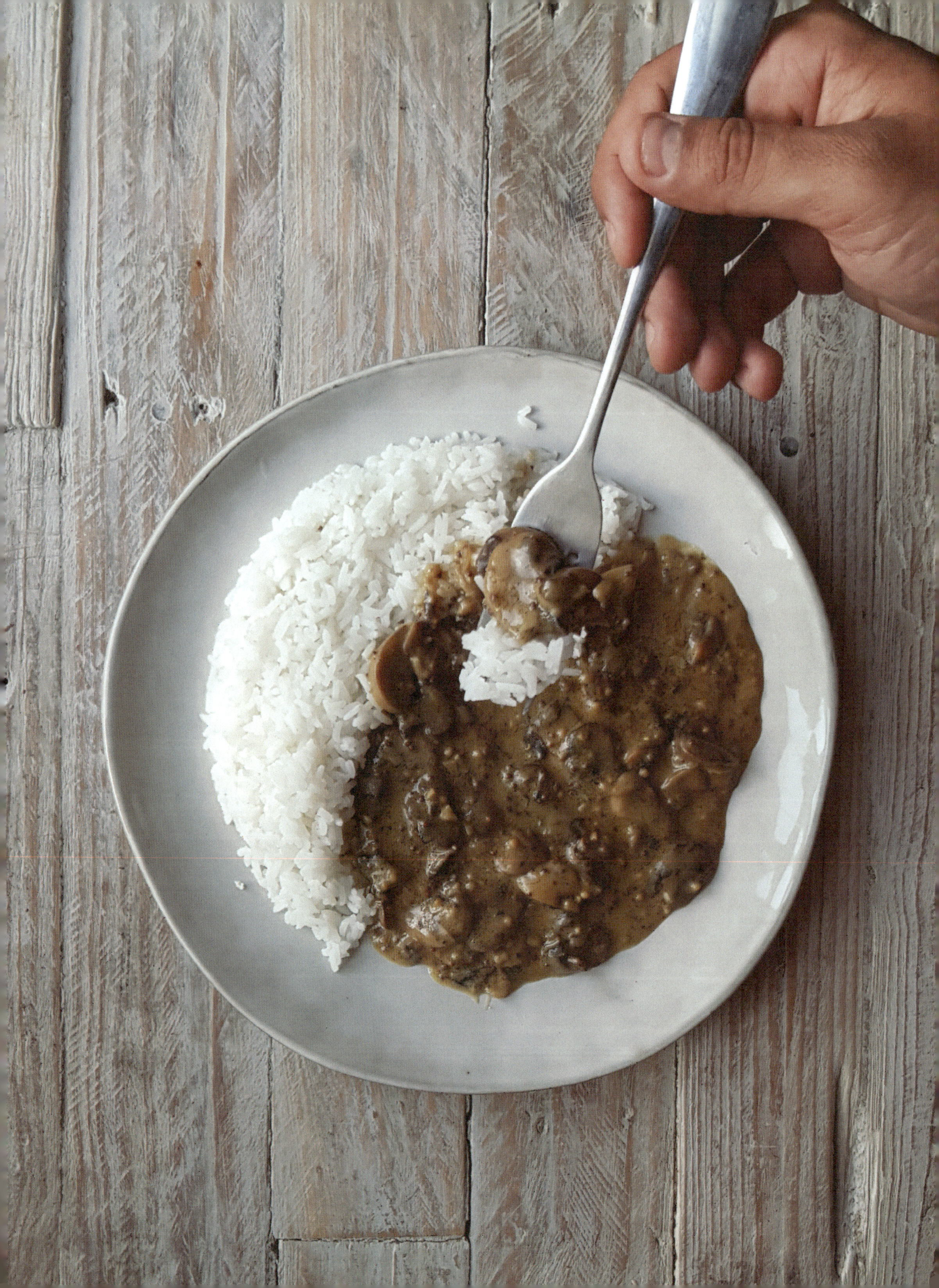

MUSHROOM STROGANOFF

SERVES: 5 | COOKING TIME: 1 HOUR

This has been a recipe that my mum made for me growing up. A perfectly creamy and tangy weekend dish that's light and delicious. This mushroom classic is bound to become a firm family favourite!

INGREDIENTS

500g mix of mushrooms *(chestnut, portobello, button)*

½ red onion

3 garlic cloves

2 tbsp vegan butter

100ml vegan white wine *(optional)*

2 tbsp wholegrain mustard

1 vegetable stock cube

300ml soy/rice milk

50ml olive oil

Salt

Black pepper

2 handfuls rice

TIME TO FEED THE SOUL

Heat the butter in a large pan and thinly slice down the onion. Once the butter is hot and melted, begin frying the onion.

Slice the garlic and add to the pan with the onions until tender. In the meantime, slice and chop down the mushrooms; you want them to be visible as the main ingredient but still be bite-size.

Next, add the mushrooms to the frying pan with the other ingredients so that they go golden and tender and release all the excess water inside them.

Once the mushrooms are cooked, mix together the mustard and vegetable stock and add this to the pan. Then, add in the cream *(mix together the soy milk and olive oil separately and blend)*.

Leave the pan to simmer on a low - medium heat for 5 minutes or so, until the sauce thickens. Finally, season with salt and pepper.

Whilst it simmers, boil some rice until tender. Serve by spooning the stroganoff mixture over the rice. Alternatively, serve with some chips. The choice is yours.

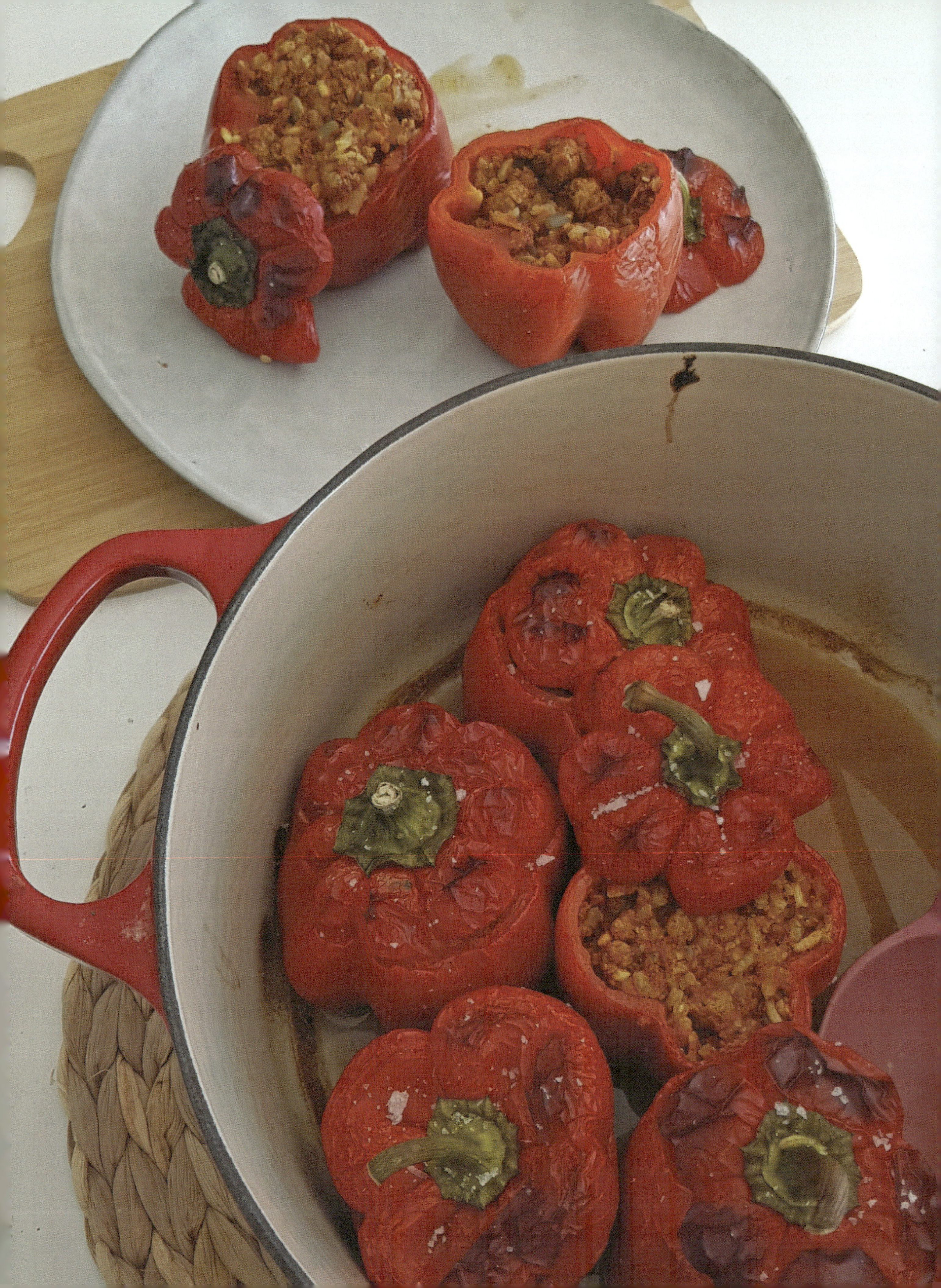

STUFFED AND ROASTED BELL PEPPERS

SERVES: 4 | COOKING TIME: 1 HOUR 30 MINUTES

Roast peppers are so deliciously sweet, and even better when you stuff them. You can keep this popular recipe cruelty-free by using vegan mince or replacing the mince with lentils to create a filling that best suits you. Don't let their looks deceive you as they are quite filling.

INGREDIENTS

- 8 bell peppers
- 250g vegan mince
- Olive oil
- 20g nut and seed mix
- 1 small onion
- 1 garlic clove
- 1 tsp cumin
- 1 tsp turmeric
- 2 tsp paprika
- ½ tsp cinnamon
- 400g tomate triturado
- 1 tbsp tomato purée
- 6 - 8 sundried tomatoes
- 100g rice
- Vegetable stock cube
- Rock salt
- Black pepper

TIME TO FEED THE SOUL

Start off by preheating your oven to 180°C and placing the rice to boil in a small pot with hot water. Cut open your peppers, keeping them whole and clean out any seeds *(keep the lids to one side for later)*. Lay out the peppers in a large casserole pot with the open bit facing up, ready for the filling to be inserted.

Making sure to dice them very small, chop up the garlic, onion, and sundried tomatoes and place them in a large pan with olive oil to slowly fry over a low - medium heat so that they caramelise.

Once the onions and the rest are looking soft and tender, add in the vegan mince and season with all the spices, salt and pepper, and cook until the mince is browned. When the filling is cooked, add the tomate triturado, tomato purée, the drained rice, and 100ml water and allow everything to stew and reduce so that all flavours combine.

Once the water has reduced, scoop the mixture into the peppers. Cover with the tops of the peppers and pour 200ml water mixed with the stock cube into the casserole dish, around the peppers.

Cover the casserole dish and transfer to the oven for 35 - 45 minutes, until the peppers are lovely and tender, remove the lid 5 - 10 minutes before to get a little charring in on top.

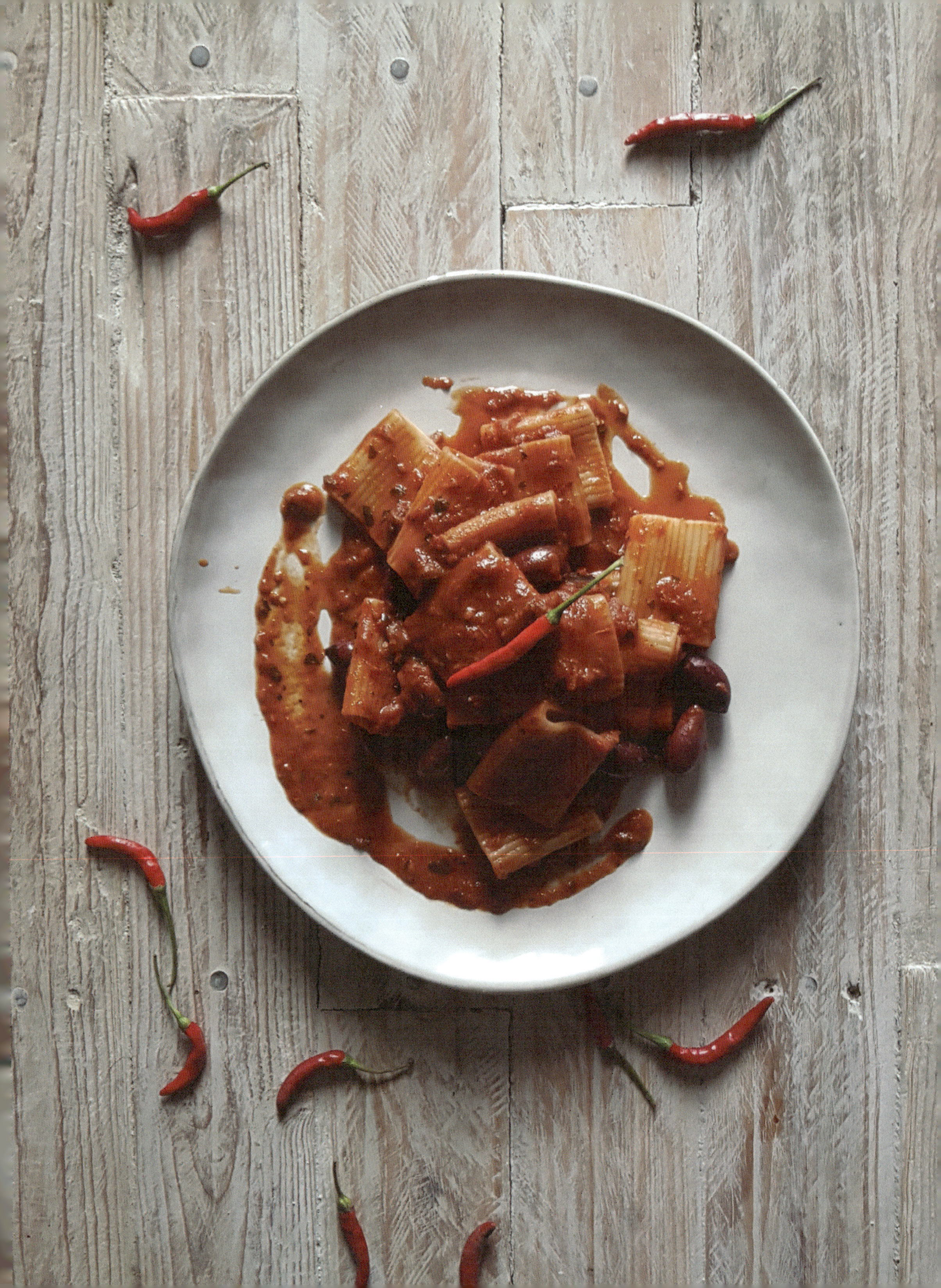

RIGATONI WITH AUBERGINE & BLACK OLIVE RAGU

Serves: 3 | Cooking Time: 45 Minutes

A balanced dish of naturally sweet flavours stewed together to achieve a rich combination of flavours that leaves you with a ragu you just want to lick off the plate.

INGREDIENTS

- Vegan rigatoni pasta
- 6 fresh tomatoes
- 2 tbsp tomato purée
- 1 garlic clove
- 1 chilli
- Black Kalamata olives
- Fresh basil
- 200ml red wine
- 1 aubergine
- Cherry tomatoes

TIME TO FEED THE SOUL

Chop down the garlic, chilli and tomatoes and fry together over a medium heat with olive oil until soft and tender. In the meantime slice your aubergine into thin chunks.

When the tomatoes and garlic have softened, grab your hand blender and purée the ingredients together into a smooth sauce. Now pour the red wine, add the aubergine, tomato purée, a few basil leaves and olives and leave to simmer and stew until the aubergines are nice and tender. This can take up to 40 minutes.

About 10 minutes before the ragu is ready, place the pasta to boil until al dente *(seasoning the pasta water with salt and a drizzle of oil)*. Use the pasta water to thin the sauce if you find that it's too thick. You can serve the pasta and Pour the ragu over the pasta, or mix the pasta in with the sauce and serve together. Finally, break a few basil leaves on top and enjoy.

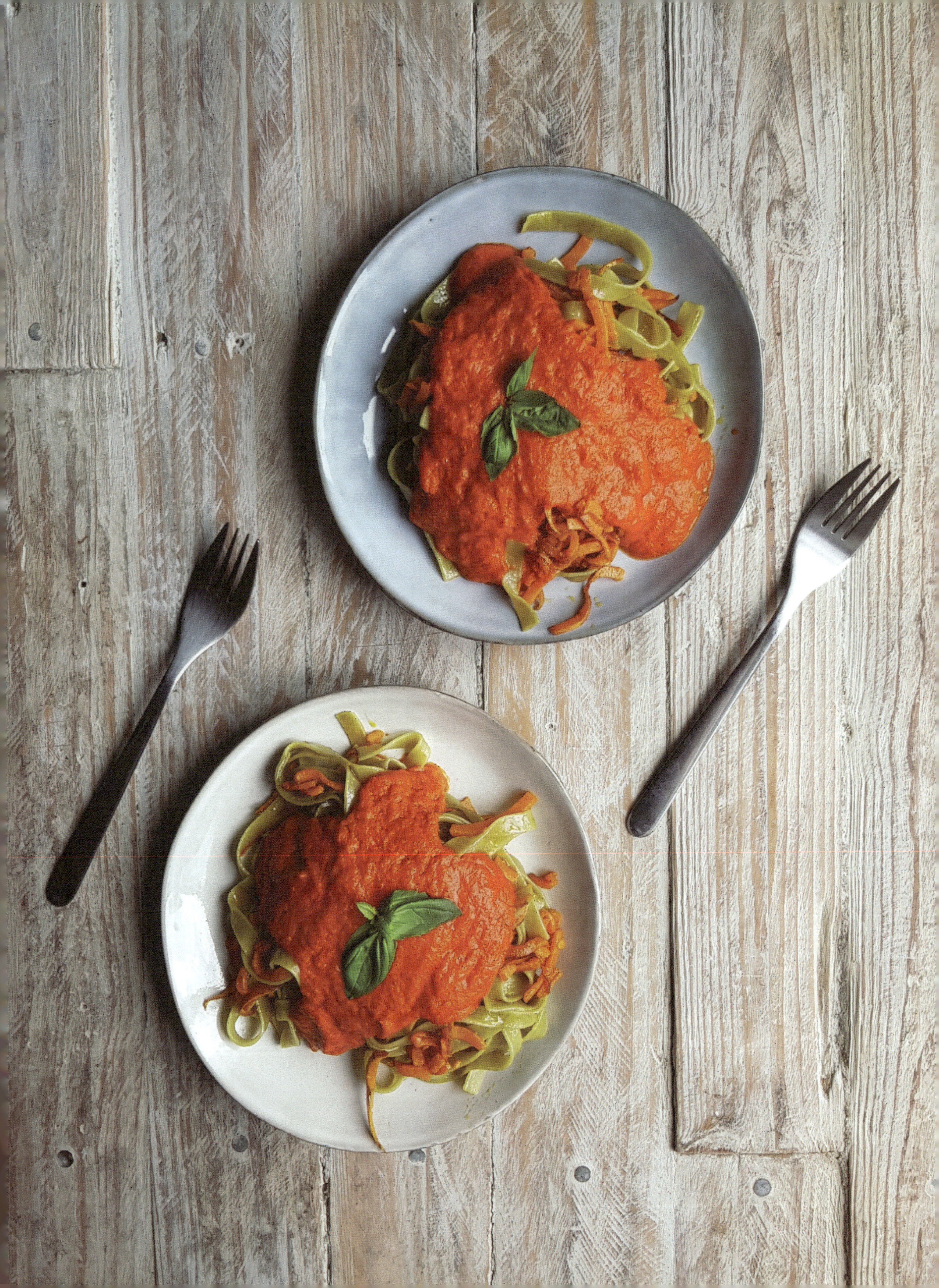

SWEET POTATO NOODLES & RED PEPPER SAUCE

Serves: 4 | Cooking Time: 1 hour 20 minutes

Have you tried a spiraliser before? It can be quite fun to play with, creating different shapes and textures out of an otherwise ordinary vegetable!

INGREDIENTS

- 1 medium courgette
- 1 large sweet potato
- Spinach tagliatelle
- 200g roasted red peppers
- 3 large tomatoes
- ½ onion
- 2 garlic cloves
- Sweet paprika
- Vegan parmesan cheese
- Olive oil
- Salt
- Black pepper
- Fresh coriander

TIME TO FEED THE SOUL

You will need to own a spiraliser to really make the most of this recipe.

Start off by preparing the sauce. If using fresh peppers then lay the peppers, tomatoes and garlic cloves out on an oven tray and drizzle with oil and salt, place them in the oven for an hour or so at 180°C until soft.

If you're using pre-roasted peppers from a jar or packet then crush the garlic, slice the onion and fry it in some oil over a medium heat along with some diced tomatoes, so that it softens and sweetens the flavour.

Place the taglietelle to boil in a pan. Whilst the sauce ingredients are cooking away, bring out your spiraliser, rinse the courgette and peel the sweet potato. Spiralise them both, season and fry them in oil in a hot pan, tossing them ocassionally as they cook.

Once the sauce ingredients are ready, blend them into a smooth sauce. Serve the sautéd potato noodles and courgettes together with the taglietelle and cover with a generous amount of sauce.

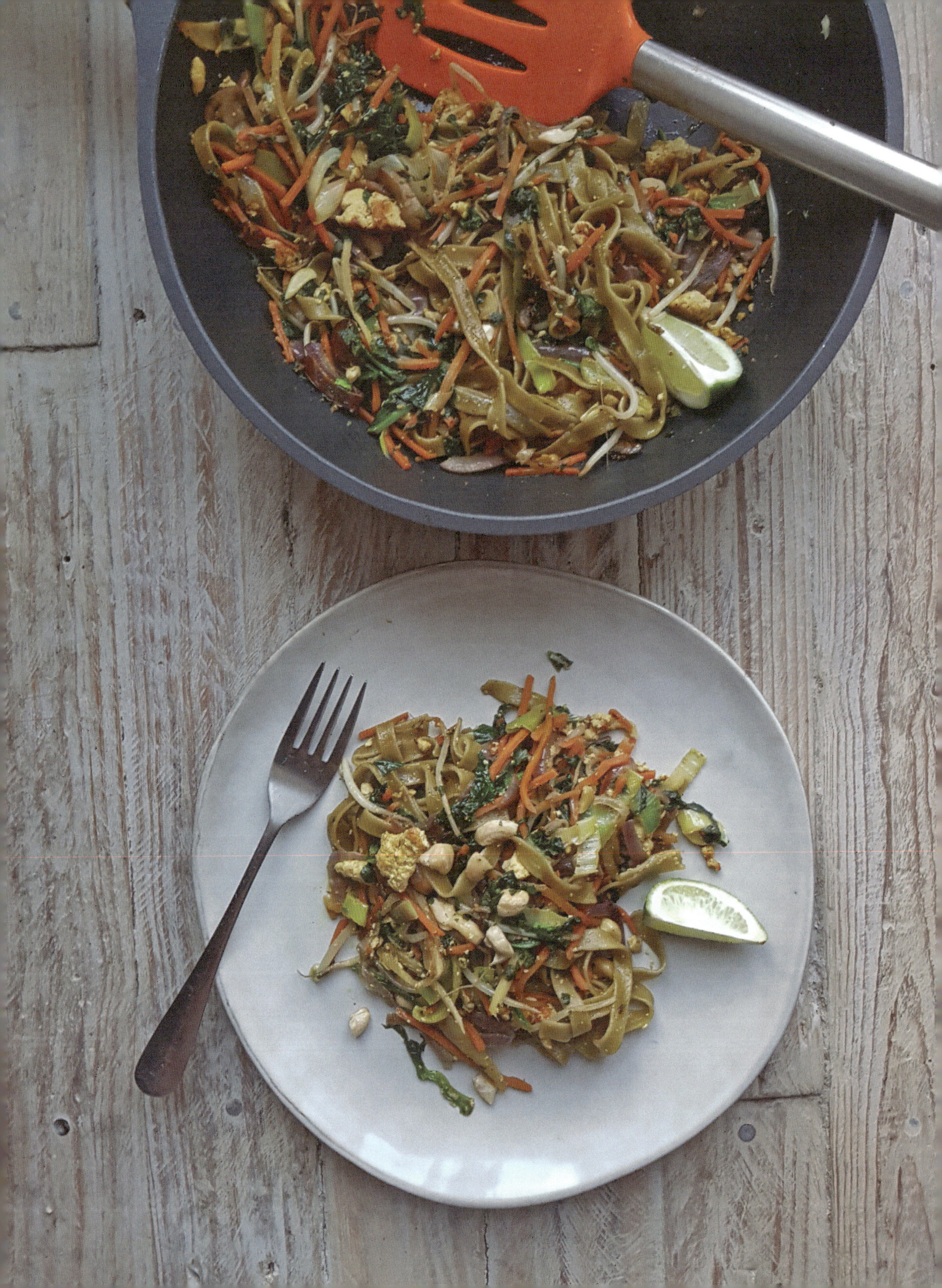

VEGAN PAD THAI

Serves: 4 | Cooking Time: 40 Minutes

I do like a good pad Thai. I mean, nothing really compares to a traditional and authentically prepared dish, but I have enjoyed adapting this one using ingredients I had lying around to get as close to the real deal as possible. try it as a savoury, satisfying dish - or be brave with the hot sauce for a fiery one with a good old kick!

INGREDIENTS

200g spinach tagliatelle

Vegan 'scrambled egg':
1 block firm tofu
½ tsp turmeric
½ tsp rock salt
1 tbsp wok oil

Sauce:
Juice of ½ lime
3 tbsp demerara sugar
2 tbsp hot sauce
3 tbsp soy sauce

Stir fry:
3 spring onions
100g bean sprouts
Raw cashews
2 garlic cloves
1 carrot
Fresh coriander
1 ginger root
Kale or lettuce leaves

TIME TO FEED THE SOUL

Start off by preparing the sauce. Mix the ingredients together in a bowl and combine. Set this to one side.

Now, slice all the ingredients, mince the garlic, and grate the carrot and peeled ginger.

Place the noodles in a bowl with boiling water and salt and leave to boil for 3 - 5 minutes until al dente.

Add a splash of oil to a large wok dish, crumble in the tofu, and fry with a sprinkling of turmeric *(for colour)*. After about 4 minutes, turning and tossing the tofu as it cooks, add a sprinkle of rock salt.

Continue by adding the vegetables to the wok and stir frying your ingredients, leaving the coriander for the end. Drizzle the vegetables with a bit of oil whilst frying and once tender, add the sauce you prepared earlier to the stir fry.

By now the noodles should be ready. Remove from the water, drain and add to the wok. Combine all the ingredients and serve.

(For a spicier pad Thai, add chilli flakes to the wok whilst cooking the vegetables.)

Finish off by sprinkling some crushed cashews on top of your pad Thai.

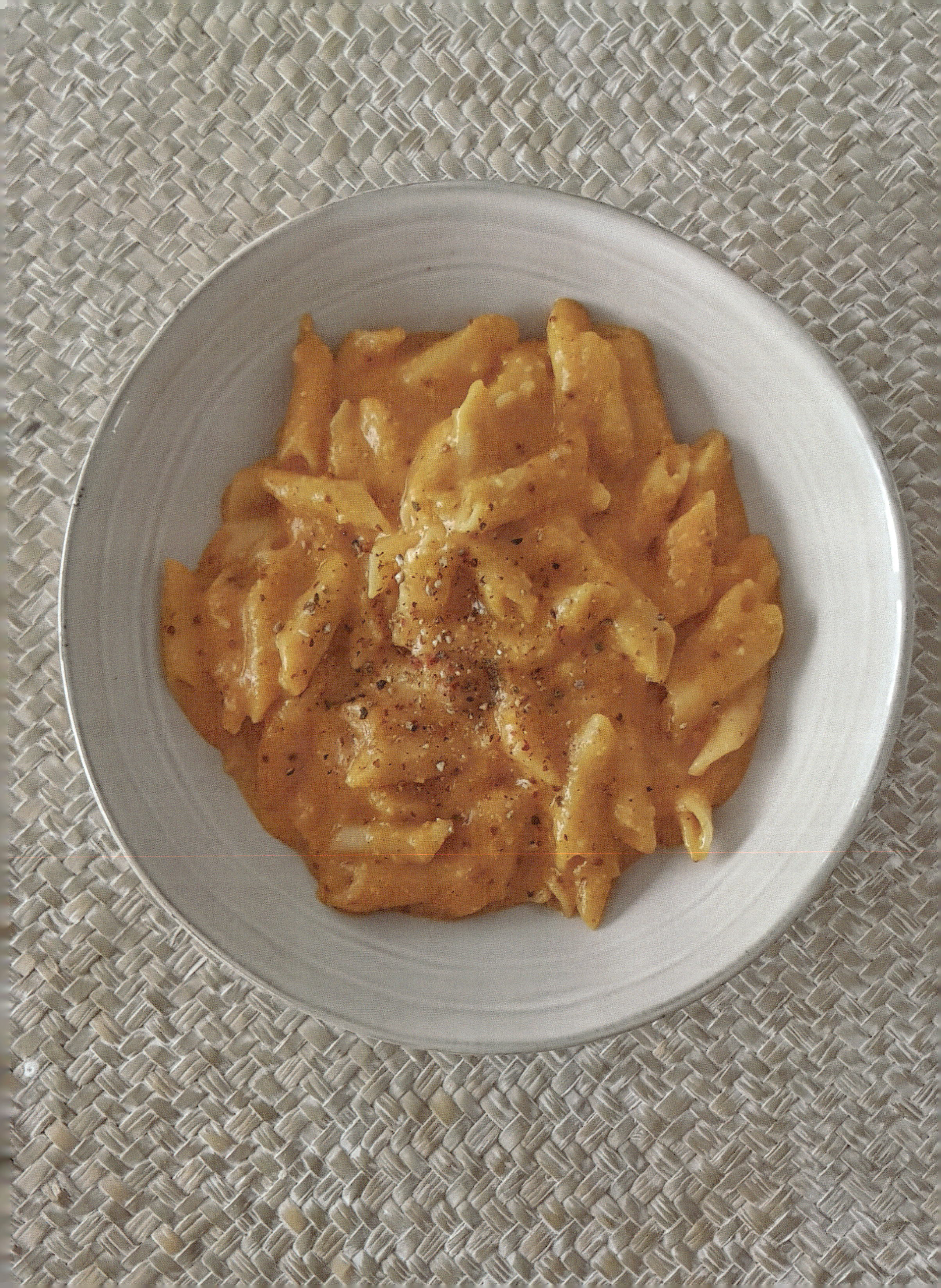

CREAMY MAC & CHEESE

Serves: 3 | Cooking Time: 30 Minutes

Growing up, mac and cheese was an exciting simple dinner that I enjoyed. What's great is that we don't actually need to use cheese to make this. Did you know that cashews make a great alternative?

Ingredients

- 225g macaroni or penne
- 100g raw cashews
- 200ml coconut milk
- 2 large potatoes
- 3 medium carrots
- ½ tsp paprika
- 2 tsp wholegrain mustard
- Pinch nutmeg
- 2 tsp cornflour *(optional)*
- Vegan cheese

Time to feed the soul

You will need two pots for this. Place your pasta in one of the pots and cover with water, leaving it to boil until al dente.

Dice the potatoes and carrots and place them into a large pot with the cashews, covering them with water and leaving them to boil over a medium heat until tender.

Once the potatoes and carrots are soft, drain all your vegetables and nuts and throw them into a food processor with a spoonful or two of the water you used to boil them in.

Purée all the ingredients in the food processor, and add the paprika, mustard and nutmeg. Blend all your ingredients together a final time. If you find the mixture too runny, slowly add in some cornflour and mix it in sufficiently bit by bit until you have a consistency you are happy with.

Drain your pasta and transfer into an oven dish. Cover with the sauce you prepared and place in the oven for 10 minutes at 200°C until golden on top.

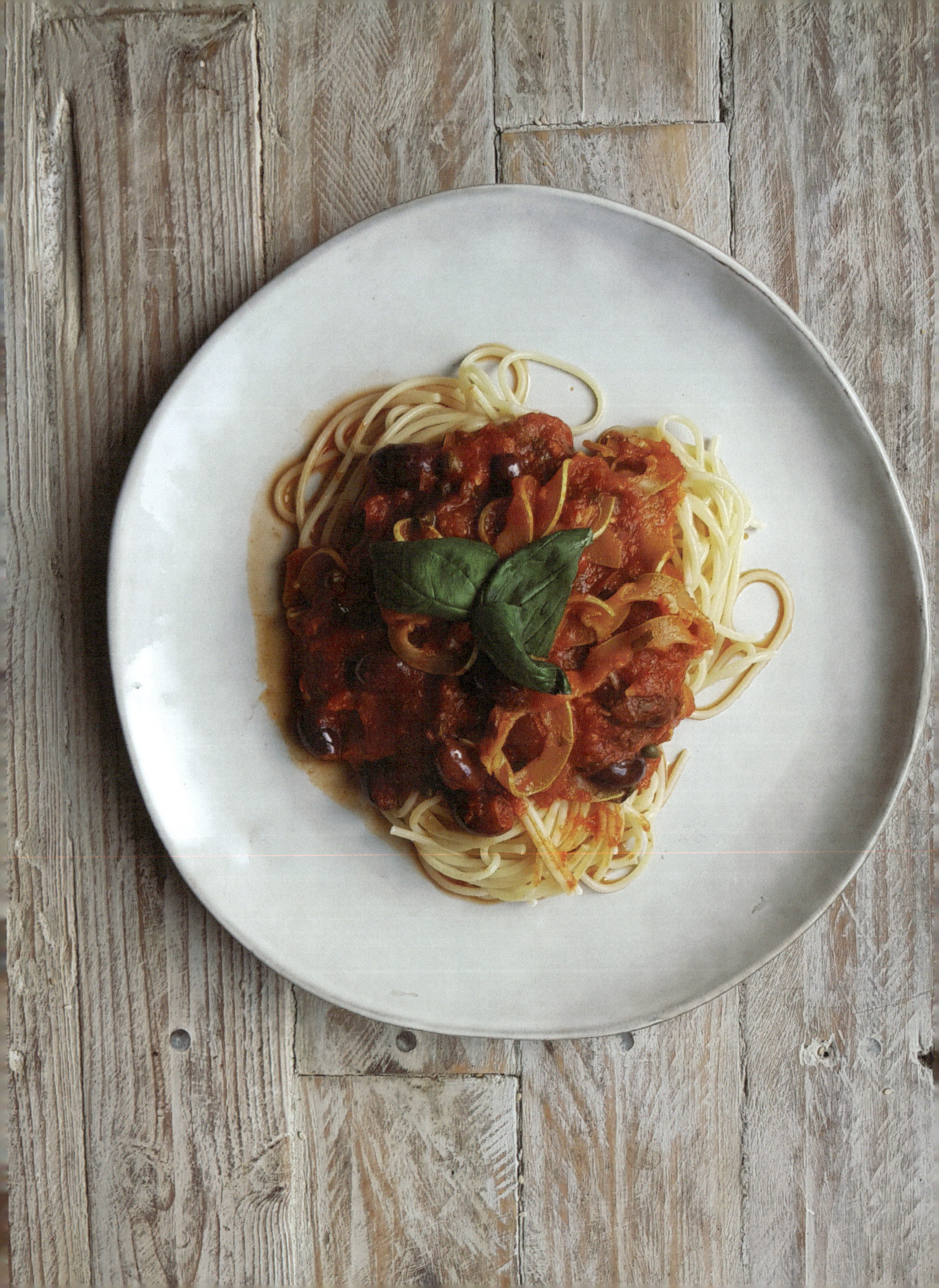

SPAGHETTI PUTTANESCA

Serves: 4 | Cooking Time: 45 Minutes

The beautiful combination of rich, sweet tomato flavours with salty ingredients balances out a pasta dish perfectly. Although this Italian classic uses anchovies to bring you a salty sea flavour, I've replaced them with capers.

INGREDIENTS

- 250g wholewheat spaghetti
- 2 courgettes *(spiralised)*
- 4 garlic cloves
- 1 medium onion
- 1 fresh tomato
- 150g Kalamata olives
- 3 tbsp capers
- 1 tsp chilli flakes
- 800g tomato sauce *(tomate triturado)*
- Fresh basil
- Fresh parsley
- Sea salt
- Black pepper
- Olive oil

TIME TO FEED THE SOUL

Boil the pasta over a medium heat.

Drizzle olive oil on the base of a separate large pan. Finely dice the onion and garlic into very small pieces and add to the pan to cook over a medium heat and stir continuously.

Once the onion and garlic have softened *(this will only take a minute or two)*, lower the heat and add a chopped up fresh tomato. Leave the ingredients to stew and the tomato to purée, stirring once in a while so that it doesn't burn. Next, add in the chilli flakes and capers, stirring everything together so that the chilli lightly fries and the capers release their saltiness, then pour in the tomato sauce.

At this point add the olives *(make sure the stones are removed)*, spiralise your courgette and add this to the pan too. *(If you don't have a spiraliser then thinly cut the courgettes into thin strips.)*

Season to taste with salt and black pepper. Finely chop down a handful of basil and parsley and add this to the saucepan. Stir everything together and leave over a medium heat for 4 - 5 minutes to combine the flavours.

If you see the sauce is reducing too much, add a spoonful of the pasta water to the sauce. Drain the pasta, and either add this to the saucepan and stir everything together, or alternatively serve the pasta and cover with generous servings of the sauce on top.

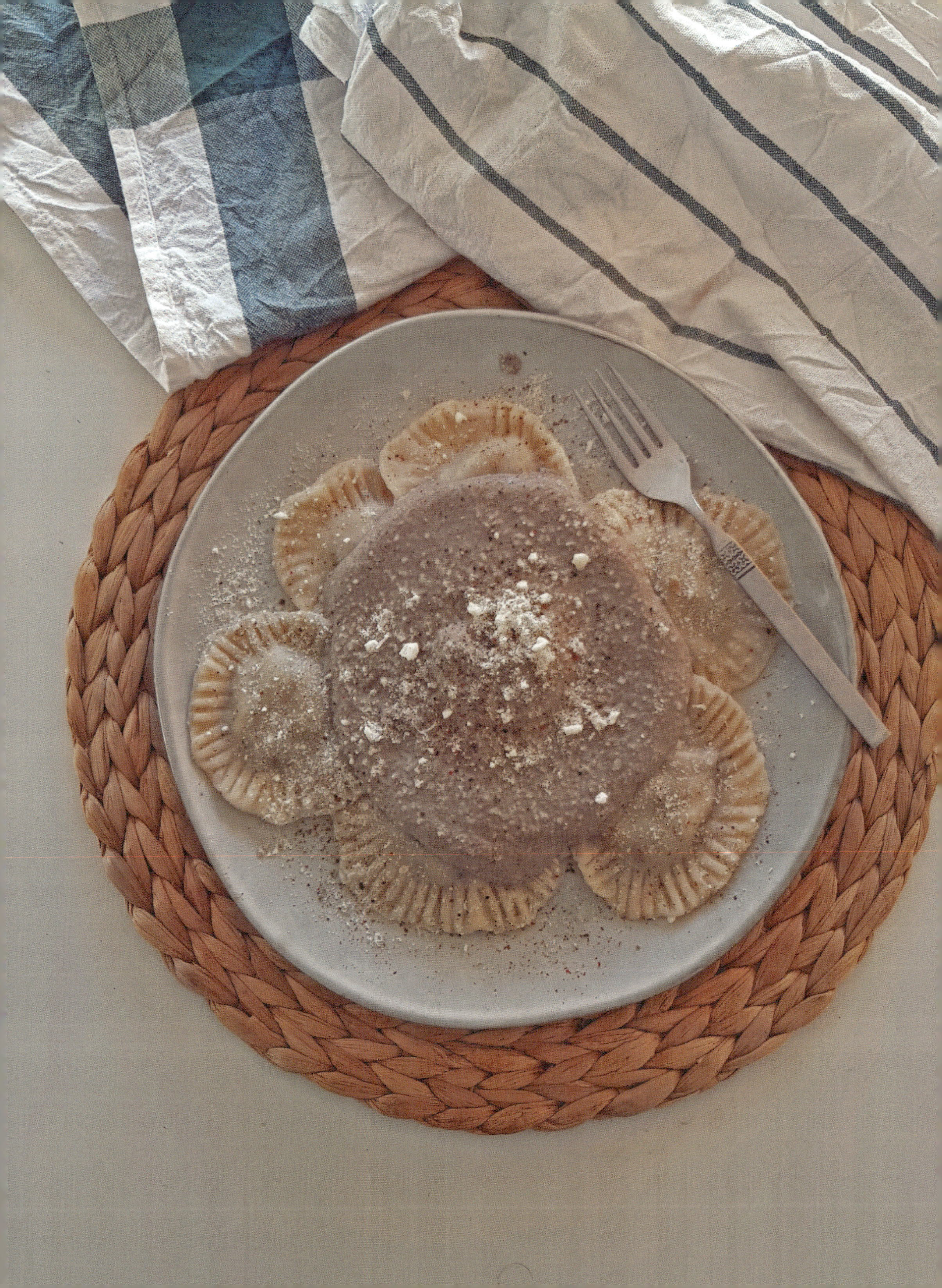

SPINACH & MUSHROOM RAVIOLI

Serves: 5 | Cooking Time: 1 Hour

There's something very rewarding about making your own pasta. The time and love that goes into each piece just makes it taste that much better. Spinach and mushroom is the filling I chose, but you can adapt the recipe to suit the ingredients you have available.

INGREDIENTS

Pasta
200g strong flour
200g semolina
2 tbsp olive oil
200ml warm water

Filling
2 garlic cloves
150g fresh spinach
Splash of white wine
2 tsp olive oil
150g vegan cream cheese*
Sea salt
6 or 7 mushrooms

Sauce
50g mushrooms
Fresh thyme
100g vegan parmesan cheese
100g coconut cream

If you cannot find vegan cream cheese then use vegan ricotta..

TIME TO FEED THE SOUL

Start off with the ravioli filling. Dice up the garlic and mushrooms and fry in olive oil with a pinch of salt until you see the mushroom has lost their water, then add a splash of white wine and toss in the spinach leaves. Fry all the ingredients together *(the spinach will release a lot of water as it cooks and reduce dramatically)*. Continue stirring as it fries.

Once everything has reduced, transfer the cooked ingredients to a food processor *(try not to transfer too much liquid whilst doing so)*, add the cream cheese, and blend until smoother but still thick.

Next, move onto the pasta dough, leaving the filling to one side to cool. Mix all the pasta ingredients together in a bowl, and knead until you have a smooth dough that doesn't stick to the sides of the bowl - it should feel slightly elastic. If you have time, cover the dough and place in the fridge for an hour to firm up slightly.

Sprinkle your surface with flour, then take half the ball of dough and roll it out thinly. Use a cookie cutter or similar object to cut even shapes - whether they are squares or circles is up to you!

Spoon a teaspoon or so of the filling into the centre of one of the dough shapes, leaving a centimetre or so of space from the edge, and brush some water along the sides of the dough, then cover with another cut-out dough shape. Press a fork along to the edges to seal.

Transfer the ravioli into a pot with boiling, salted water, and boil for 3 minutes until they float.

Prepare the sauce by slicing and frying the mushrooms then adding the coconut cream and cheese.

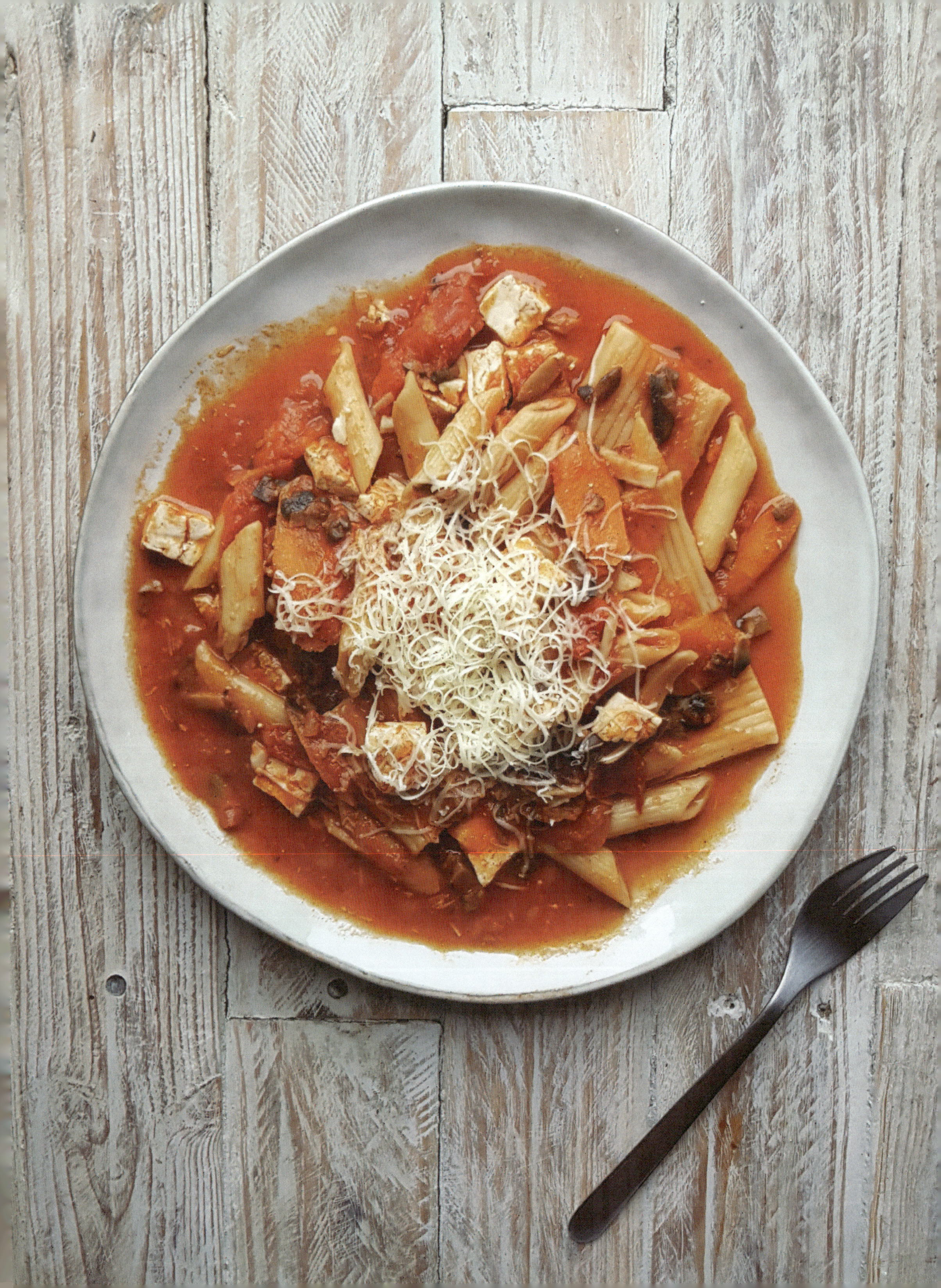

MAMA'S VEGAN ROSTO

Serves: 5 | Cooking Time: 1 Hour

This classic Gibraltar favourite is a staple dish in most households. This incredibly rich tomato based dish takes its inspiration from Gibraltar's Genoese heritage. Replace the meat with the a vegan substitute and you have a dish almost identical to the original.

INGREDIENTS

- 200g chestnut mushrooms
- 300g rigatoni or penne pasta
- 200g vegan Quorn or extra firm tofu
- 100ml vegetable stock
- 1 jar baby potatoes
- 400g tinned tomatoes *(triturado)*
- 1 tbsp tomato puree
- ½ tsp sugar
- 1 small onion
- 3 large tomatoes
- 2 small garlic cloves
- 3 small carrots *(peeled & sliced)*
- Olive oil
- ½ glass white wine *(dry)*

TIME TO FEED THE SOUL

Finely chop the onion and garlic into small pieces and fry in a large pan with olive oil. Once this is softening slice tomatoes and add to the pan with the onion and garlic. When the ingredients are tender and cooked, blend them together using a hand blender, then slice the carrots and add them to the sauce.

Cut the mushrooms in half and dice the Quorn/tofu into small pieces. Once the rest of the ingredients are soft, add these two to the pan, add an extra splash of oil and sauté with the rest of the ingredients for a couple of minutes.

Now pour the tinned tomatoes and potatoes into the pan and add the tomato puree, sugar, vegetable stock or dissolved vegetable stock cube, and the white wine to the pan. Stir all your ingredients and leave, covered, to simmer for 15 - 20 minutes to allow the sauce to reduce.

In a separate pan, pour some boiling water and boil the past until al dente. Once ready drain and pour into the pan with the rest of the ingredients.

Allow 5 - 10 minutes for the flavours to mix together and settle.

(And like lasagne, I think Rosto always tastes better the next day.)

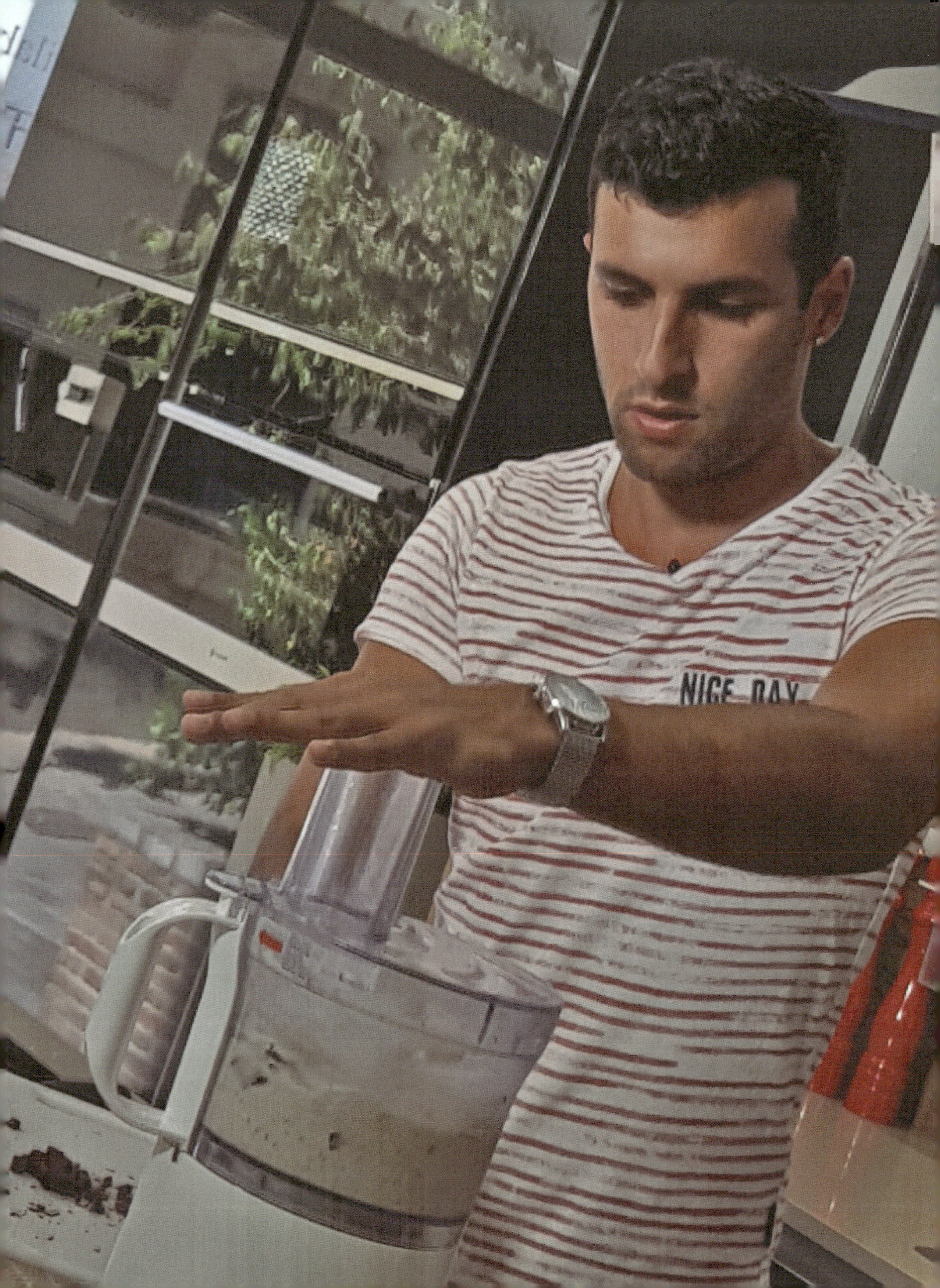
NICE DAY

The Sweet Treats

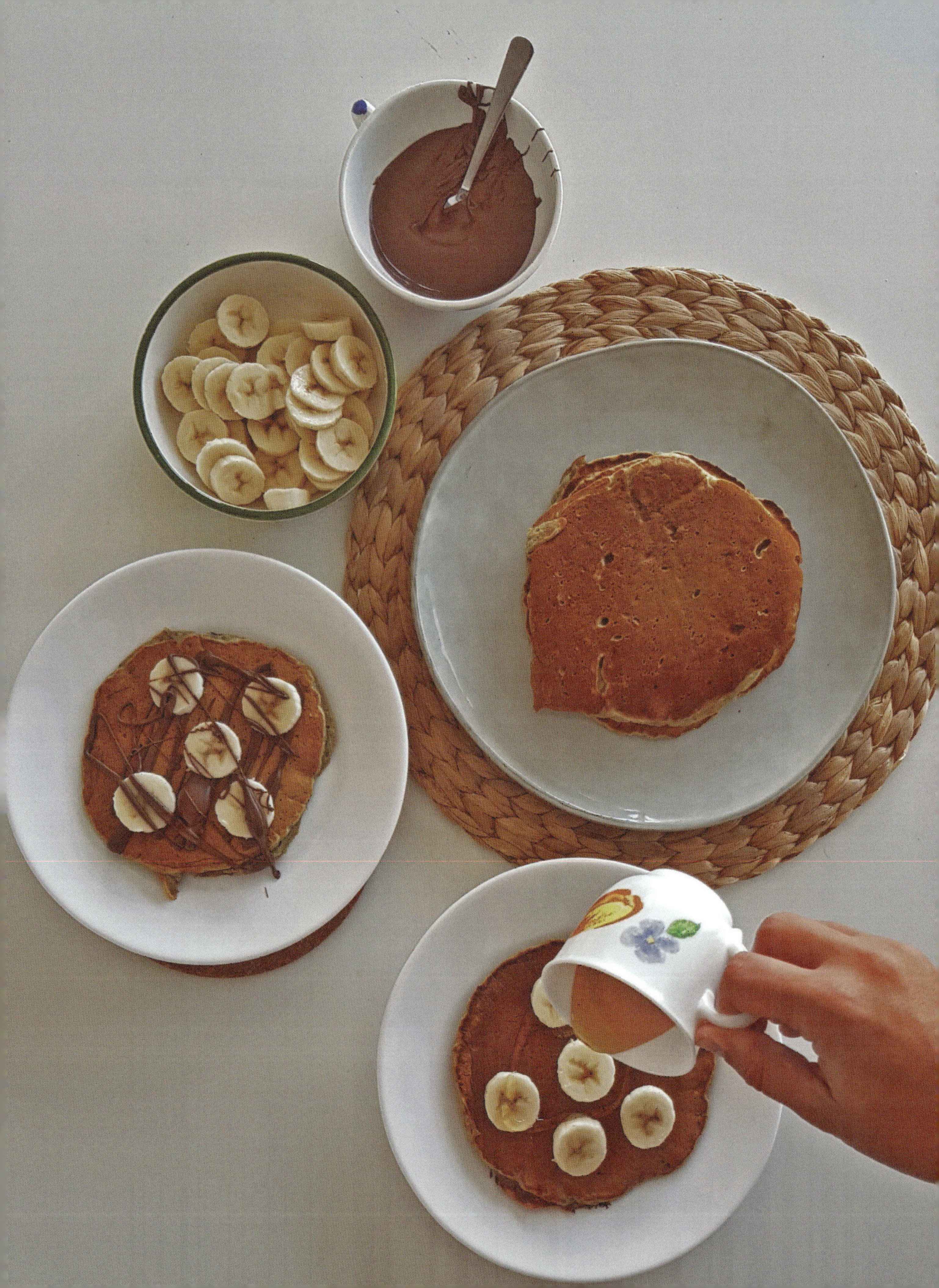

BANANA PANCAKES

Serves: 3 | Cooking Time: 20 Minutes

What could be better than waking up to the glorious smell of pancakes on a Sunday morning, whilst the sun shines in through the window? Well, now you can enjoy your Sunday brunch dream with your own vegan version, swapping out the egg for mashed banana.

INGREDIENTS

Pancakes
- 150g flour
- 1tsp baking powder
- 2 overripe bananas
- 200ml almond milk

Topping suggestions
- Maple syrup or agave syrup
- Strawberries
- Blueberries
- Banana
- Dark chocolate

TIME TO FEED THE SOUL

You will need to prepare the pancake ingredients separately. In one bowl mix together the dry ingredients, and in a separate bowl mash together peeled bananas, into a paste.

Add the milk to the bananas and stir together. Once runny, mix this with the dry ingredients so that you have a relatively creamy mixture.

It's important to use a medium-sized non-stick pan for these. Place the pan over a medium heat. Once hot, ladle a generous amount of the mixture into the centre of the pan.

Cook one side of the pancake. It will begin to bubble and the edges will stiffen a little. After a minute or so, using a spatula flip the pancake over and cook the opposite side. Leave to cook for another minute or so, until it turns golden.

Slide your cooked pancakes onto a plate and repeat the process with the rest of the batter to create your pancake tower.

The toppings can be adapted to your own liking. Using the bain-marie method, melt some dark chocolate in a bowl over boiling water and drizzle this over your pancakes. If you don't fancy chocolate, syrup makes a great alternative. This will add the perfect sweetness to your pancakes. Finish by topping with your favourite fruit.

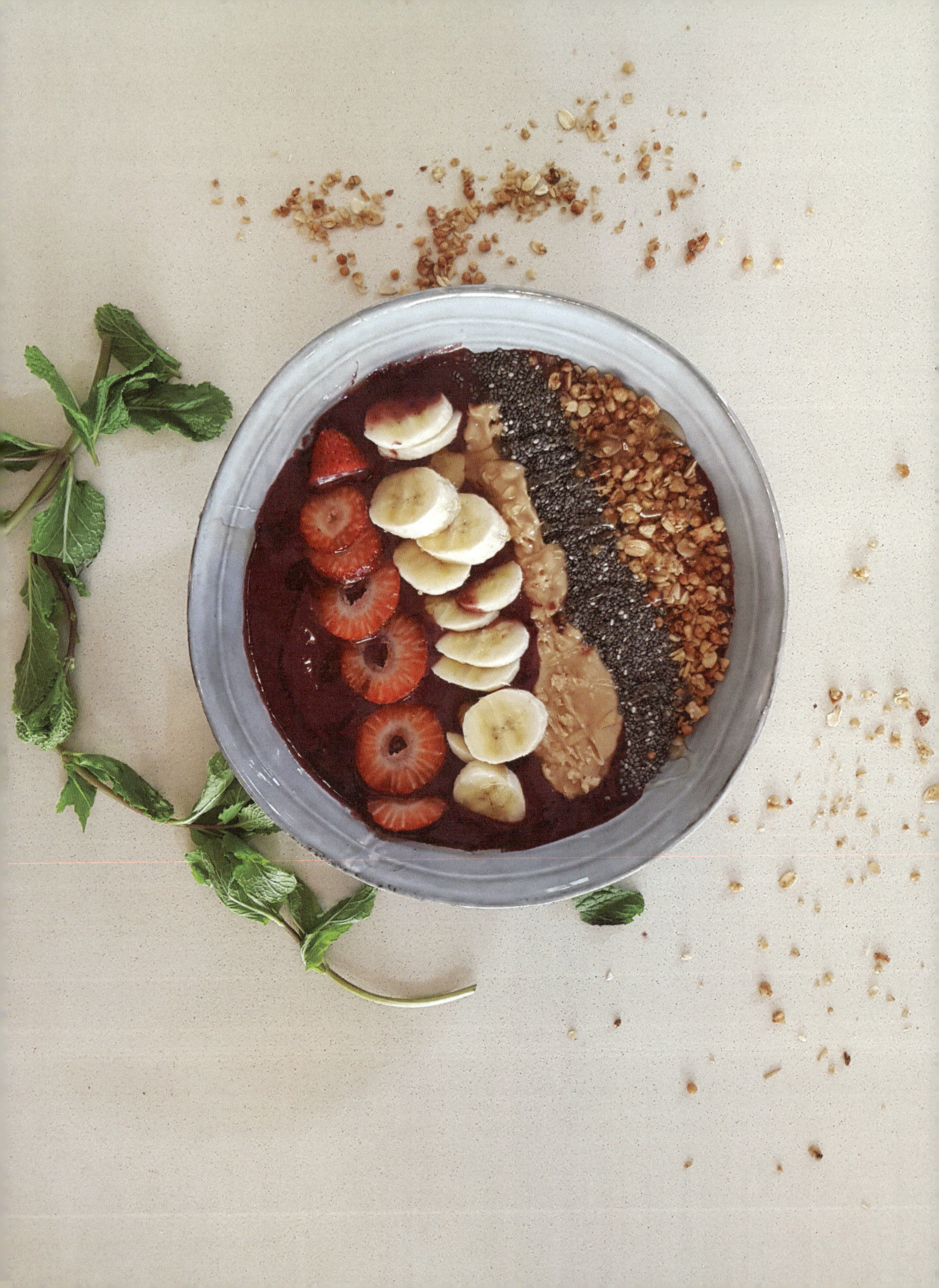

SUMMER BERRY SMOOTHIE BOWL

SERVES: 2 | COOKING TIME: 20 MINUTES

It's often said that breakfast is the most important meal of the day, bit it can also be the busiest, so why not keep it easy with a smoothie bowl? The best part is you can tweak your toppings to suit your mood.

INGREDIENTS

- 300ml coconut water
- 2 bananas
- 250g summer berries fruit mix *(strawberries, raspberries, blackberries, blueberries, etc.)*
- 1 tsp agave nectar
- Juice of ½ lemon

Topping:
- Banana
- Strawberries
- Peanut butter
- Chia seeds
- Granola

TIME TO FEED THE SOUL

Place all the smoothie ingredients in a large blender and mix together until you have a wonderfully smooth consistency.

Transfer the smoothie mix into a bowl and layer the topping ingredients. If you want a sweeter bowl then swirl some agave syrup over the top.

You can adjust the smoothie ingredients to suit the season. If you can't find any seasonal fruit to your liking, try some frozen fruit!

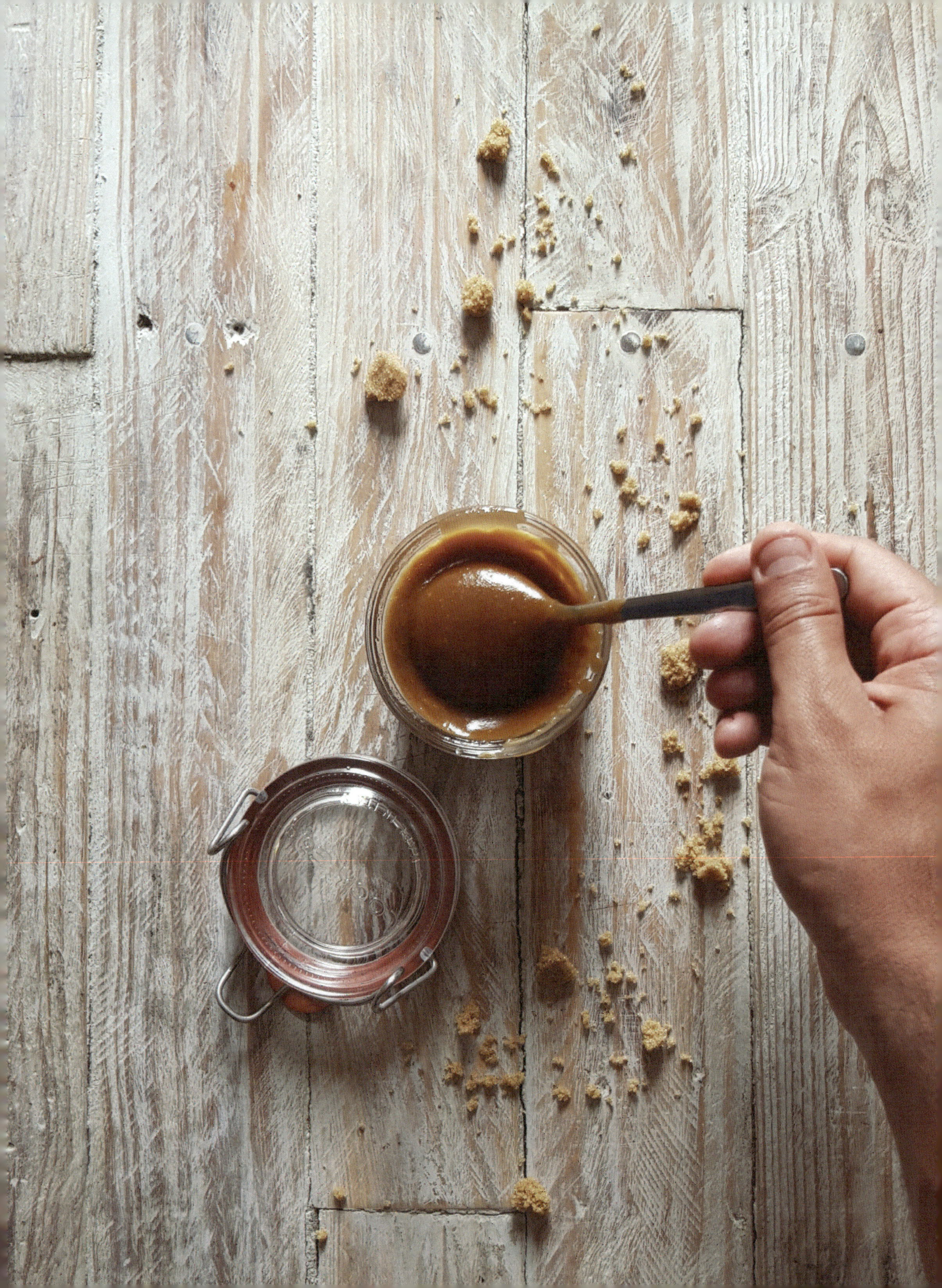

VEGAN FUDGE CARAMEL

COOKING TIME: 40 MINUTES

Making your own caramel may seem a little daunting, especially the process of melting sugar without burning it - let alone trying to make it vegan without cream! Luckily, I've cracked the caramel code for you; this recipe is sure to put a smile on your face. Use the caramel to drizzle on anything you want - fulfill your caramel dreams.

INGREDIENTS

60g coconut oil
45g maple syrup
2 tbsp vegan butter
200g light brown sugar
100ml coconut cream

Optional seasoning:
1 tsp sea salt
1 tsp cinnamon
1 vanilla pod

TIME TO FEED THE SOUL

Warm up your coconut oil in a small saucepan over a low heat and combine it with the maple syrup. Add in the vegan butter and light brown sugar and stir this continuously until the ingredients heat up, melt and combine.

When the mixture has combined and the sugar starts to pull away from the pan, add in the coconut milk and continue to stir. Bring it to a fast boil then remove from the heat and stir until cooler.

If you want a fancier caramel with a bit more 'oomph' then sneak in some salt, cinnamon or the inside of a vanilla pod. Just stir this into the mixture and you're done.

This may stiffen when it cools because of the coconut oil, so just heat it up for a few seconds before you use it until you have a viscous mixture once again.

P.S. If you put it in the fridge it goes stiff like fudge.

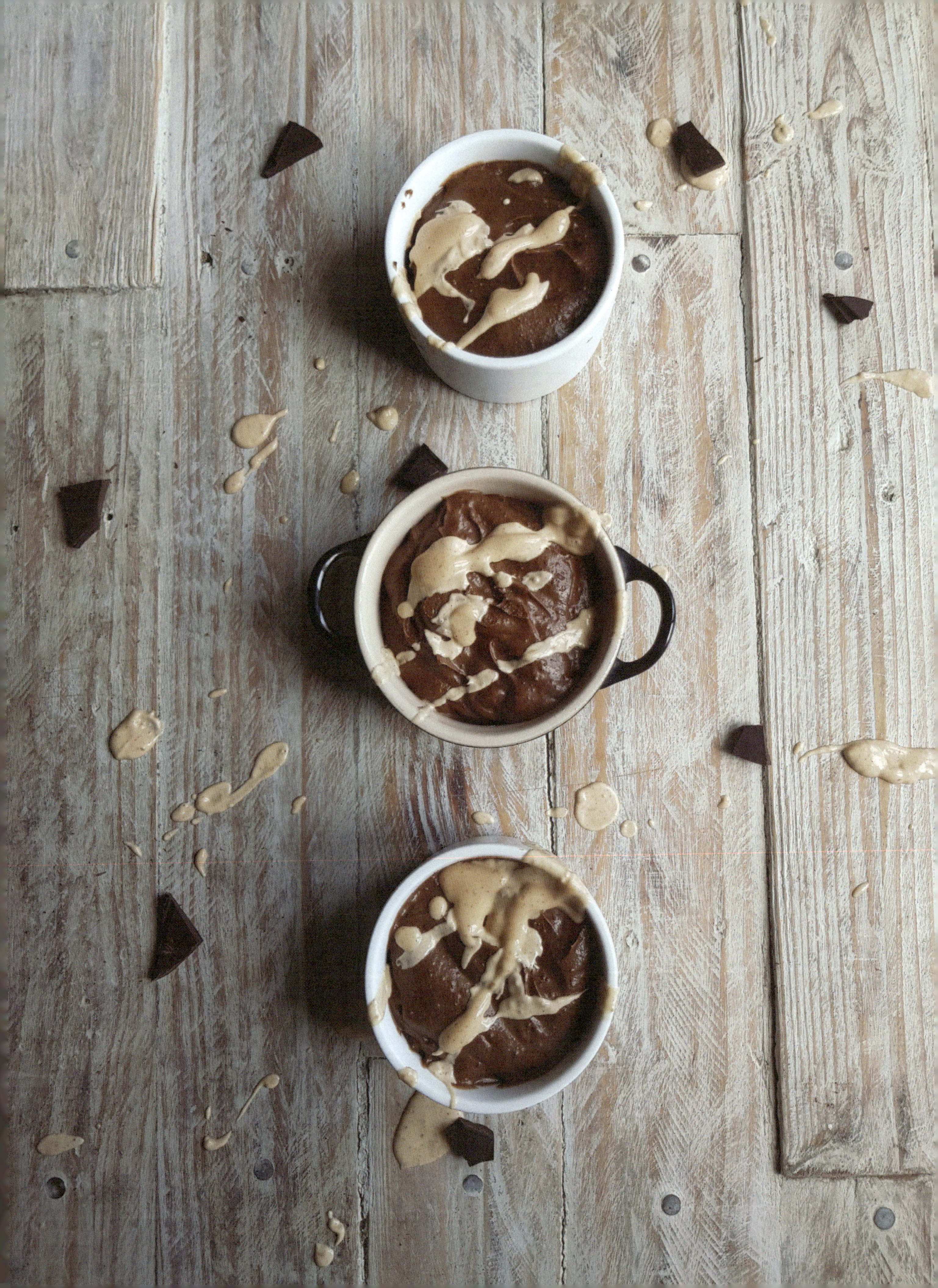

CHOCOLATE, AVOCADO & PEANUT BUTTER MOUSSE POTS

SERVES: 4 | PREPARATION: 25 MINUTES

Avocados make a great base for this recipe as they don't alter the taste of the chocolate and provide that fluffy whipped cream texture that makes mousse so desirable. Finish it off with a little salty savouriness for a rich and indulgent dessert.

INGREDIENTS

- 1 ½ bananas
- 2 avocados
- 120g peanut butter
- 100g dark chocolate
- 1 tbsp cocoa powder
- 200g maple syrup/treacle
- 100ml almond milk
- Salt flakes
- 50ml coconut cream

TIME TO FEED THE SOUL

Make sure your avocados are ripe. Cut them open in half, remove the stone and scoop out the insides into a bowl, discarding the skin.

Melt your chocolate until smooth and creamy and let it cool down a bit. Add all the ingredients into a blender except for the salt flakes and coconut cream and blend together until creamy. Taste test the blend and adjust the sweetness if need be by adding more maple syrup until you are happy with it.

Transfer the runny mousse into various pots and cover tightly with a cloth or cling film to prevent a skin forming on top. Allow to sit in the fridge for a few hours to fully set.

When ready to serve, mix together 50ml coconut cream with two tablespoons of peanut butter until combined. Drizzle over your pots and finish off with a sprinkle of sea salt on top.

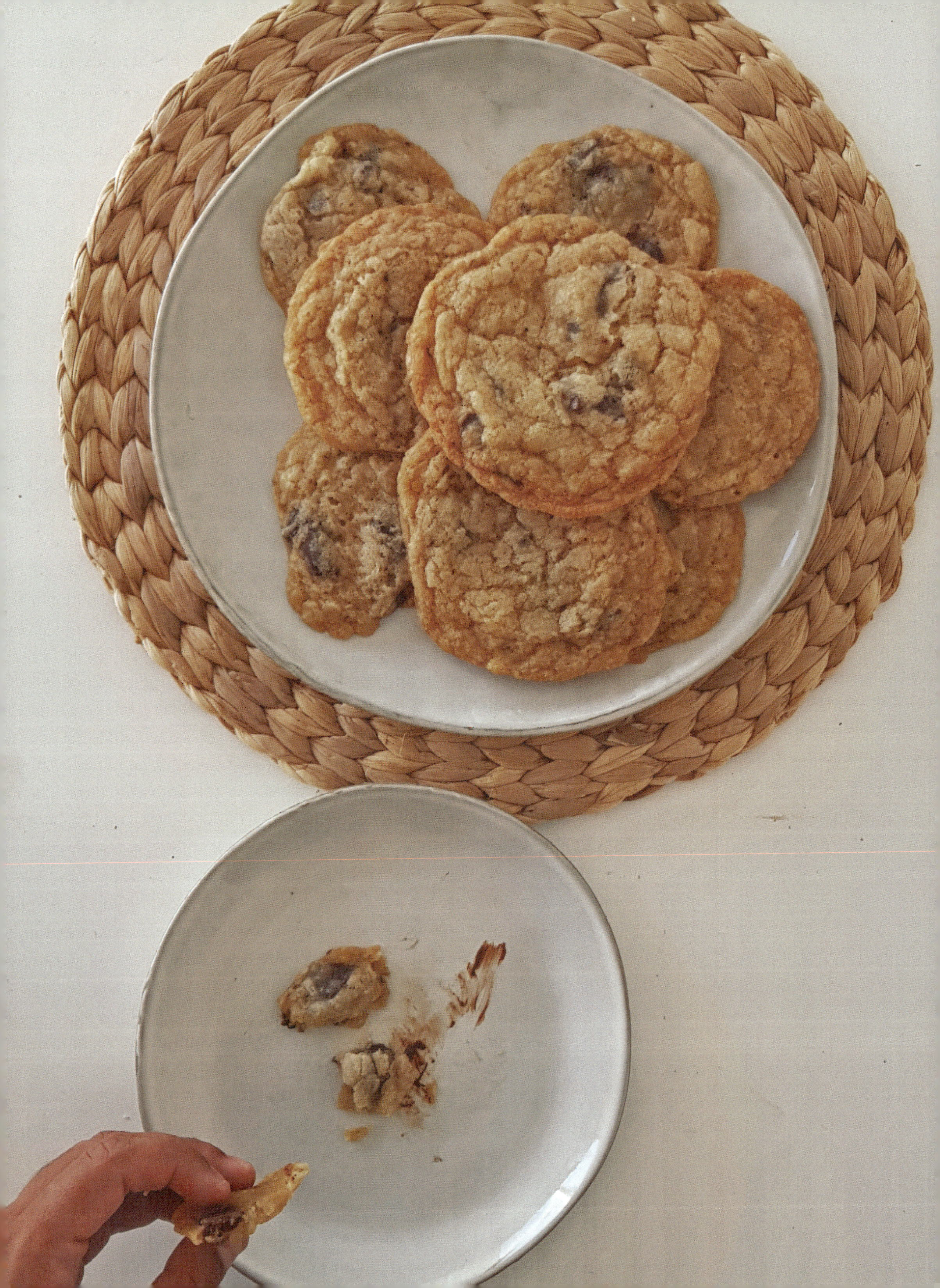

VEGAN CHOCOLATE COOKIES

SERVES: 5 | COOKING TIME: 1 HOUR

The smell of warm, freshly baked cookies as you walk into a room just makes you feel like everything is right with the world, doesn't it? Get the family involved in the process of baking these soft, chewy cookies.

INGREDIENTS

- 110g coconut oil
- 80g caster sugar
- 180g light brown sugar
- 2 tsp vanilla extract
- 100ml coconut cream
- 200g self-raising flour
- 100g dark chocolate

TIME TO FEED THE SOUL

Mix together the wet ingredients and combine until smooth. Then add the dry ingredients into the mixture a bit at a time to avoid making a mess and mix using a wooden spoon.

Chill the batter for 30 minutes to stiffen it up and make it better to manipulate.

Preheat oven to 180ºC.

Using the wooden spoon and a separate spoon to assist you, transfer several dollops of the mixture onto a greaseproof paper lined baking tray, leaving generous spaces between them as the cookies will expand.

Bake in the oven for 20 - 25 minutes, until golden. *Allow these to cool before eating them so that they can firm up as they may be quite soft when warm.*

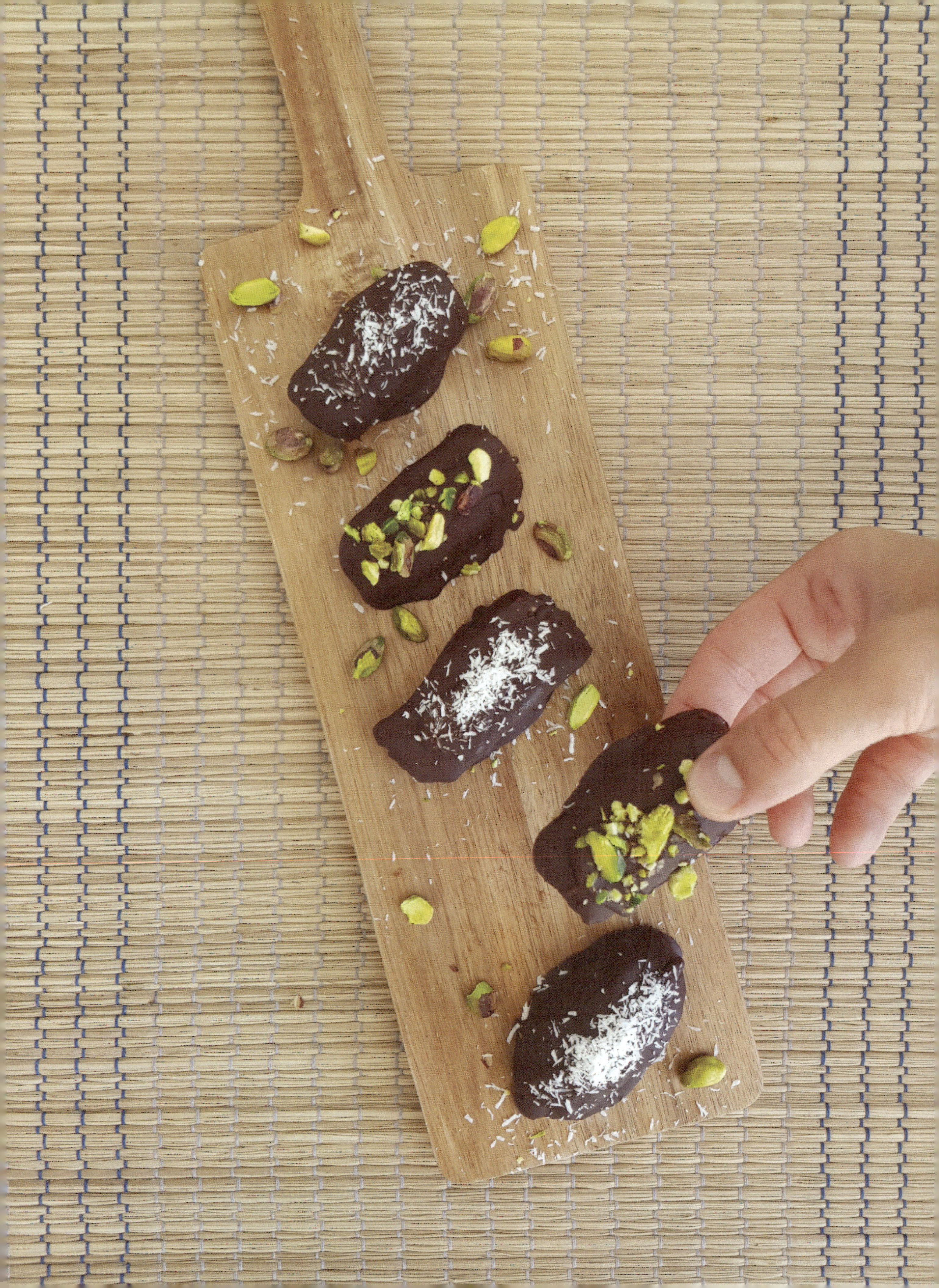

VEGAN COCO BARS

Serves: 4 | Cooking Time: 1 Hour

These light coconut bites are so delicate they just dissolve in your mouth, and the melted chocolate coating makes this a decadent and indulgent tea time snack.

INGREDIENTS

- 130g shredded coconut
- 1 tbsp powdered sugar
- 1 tbsp coconut oil
- 60ml full-fat coconut cream
- Dark melting chocolate *(vegan)*
- Pistachios

TIME TO FEED THE SOUL

Begin by combining the shredded coconut and sugar, using a spoon to mix it evenly.

Now it's time to add the wet ingredients. Pour in the coconut oil and cream and mix together until you have a paste. Using your hands, combine all the ingredients and shape them into balls or bars. Lay these out on a baking parchment.

Transfer the laid out parchment to the fridge and leave the coconut shapes to stiffen whilst you melt the chocolate.

Slowly melt the chocolate until smooth and runny; add a tablespoon of coconut oil to the chocolate if you want it runnier.

Remove your coconut shapes from the fridge, and use two forks to dip them into the chocolate, fully coating them.

Crush some pistachios or your favourite nuts and sprinkle them on top.

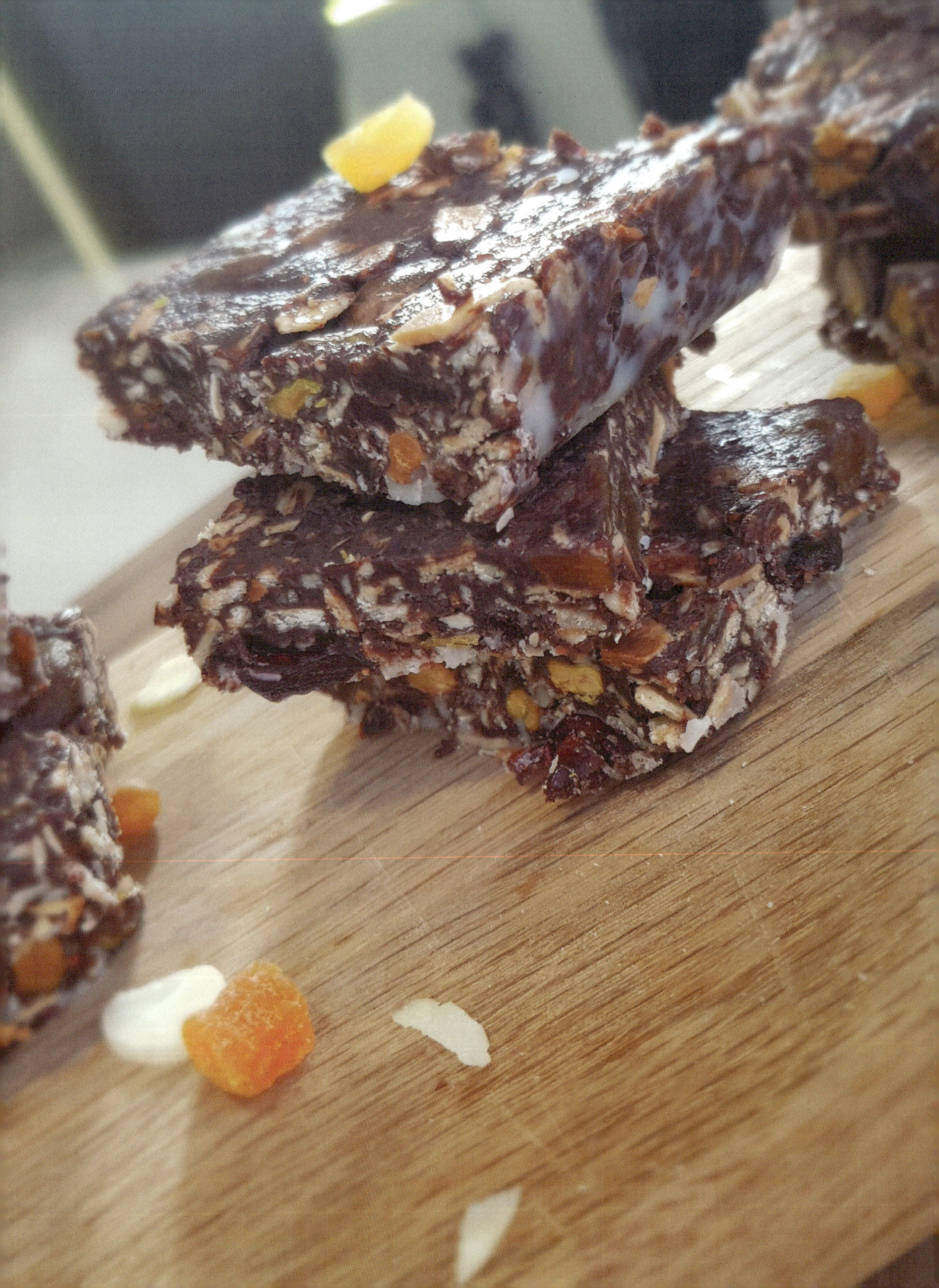

FRUITY 'ROCKY ROAD'

Serves: 4 | Cooking Time: 40 Minutes

Prepare yourself a snack that you can enjoy on the go. This recipe is all natural and quenches that afternoon craving when you're looking for that little sweet treat without the guilty feeling at the end. Packed with protein and fibres to keep your belly happy.

INGREDIENTS

- 150g fresh cranberries
- 100g pistachios
- 100g almonds
- 35g cocoa powder
- 150g – 200g coconut oil
- 100g granola and oats
- 50g dried apricots and sultanas/mixed peel

TIME TO FEED THE SOUL

Spread the pistachios and almonds out on a baking tray and toast them in the overn under a medium heat for 5 to 10 minutes.

Pour the cranberries into a pot and boil them for 10 minutes, whilst the nuts are toasting. After 10 minutes remove the nuts from the oven and drain the cranberries to remove the water.

Now blend together the cranberries and coconut oil and slowly add in the cocoa powder at the same time. *(It doesn't look great, but trust me.)*

Once smooth, transfer to a large bowl and add the nuts, the mixed peel, dried apricots and the granola to the bowl.

When everything is mixed well, line a square baking dish with greaseproof paper and squish your mixture evenly into your dish. Leave in the freezer for a few hours to stiffen. Remove 5 minutes before serving and cut into small squares.

The coconut oil keeps these firm when cool, and soft as they warm up - the perfect chewy little snack.

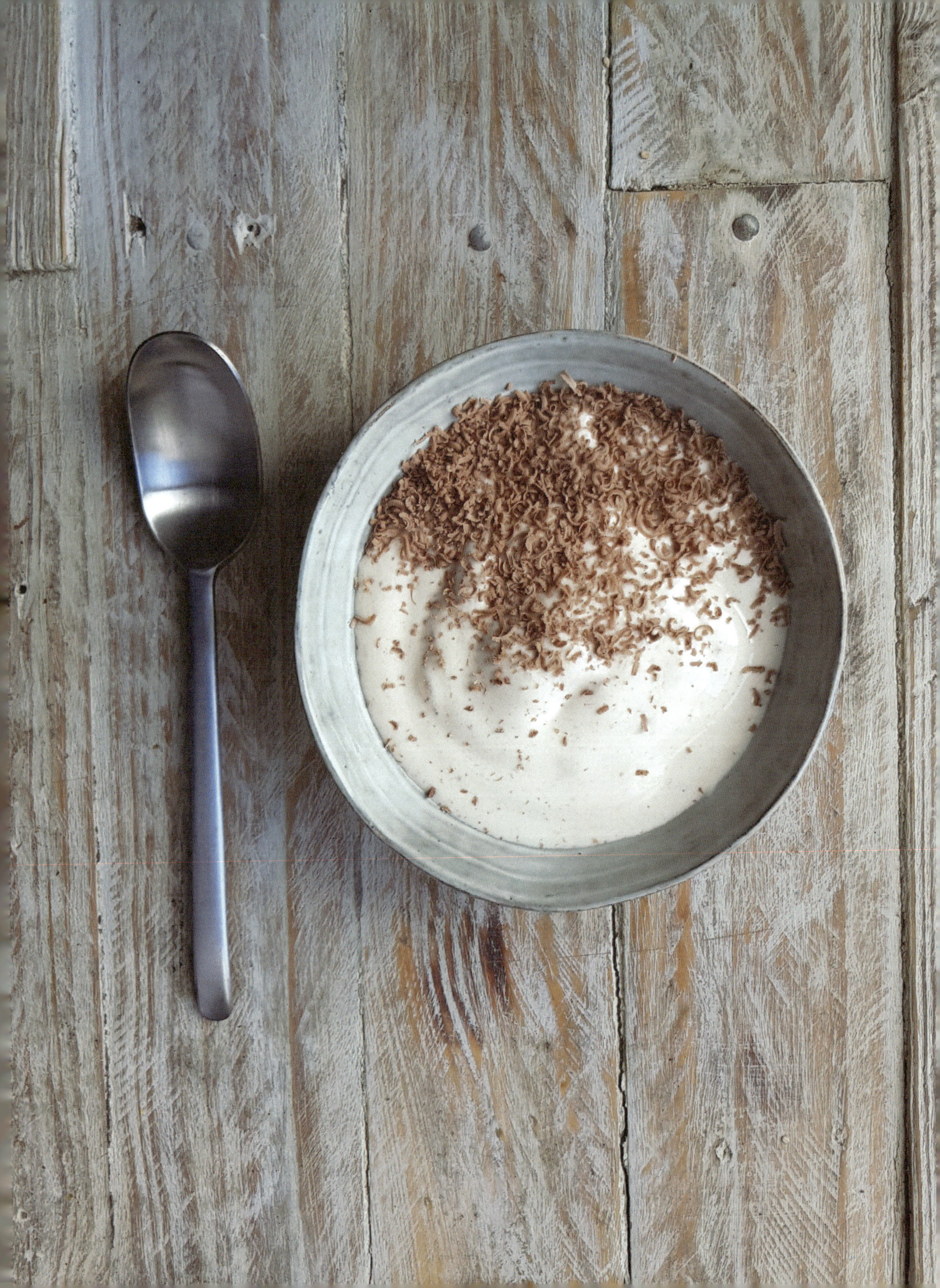

BANANA, COCONUT & CHOCOLATE ICE CREAM

SERVES: 3 | COOKING TIME: 15 MINUTES

If you know me by now then you would know I love a good sweet treat. Truth be told, I don't think there's a simpler dessert recipe than this one. Whip up a batch to keep you nice and cool in the summer.

INGREDIENTS

- 5 – 6 bananas
- 300ml coconut cream
- 100g 70% dark chocolate

TIME TO FEED THE SOUL

Peel and chop the bananas and place them in the freezer overnight or for a few hours before until entirely frozen.

Remove them from the freezer 20 minutes before making your ice cream and add the bananas to a food processor. Give them a few spins to break them down until crumbly then pour in your coconut cream and continue to blend until you have a smooth puree mixture.

Roughly chop your chocolate and add a few into the ice-cream mixture. Finish off by serving with a chocolate sprinkling on top.

If you find that the ice cream is too runny after blending, then pour it into a container and leave it in the freezer a little while to stiffe. You can then scoop it out afterwards and enjoy, like you would with any ice cream. YUM.

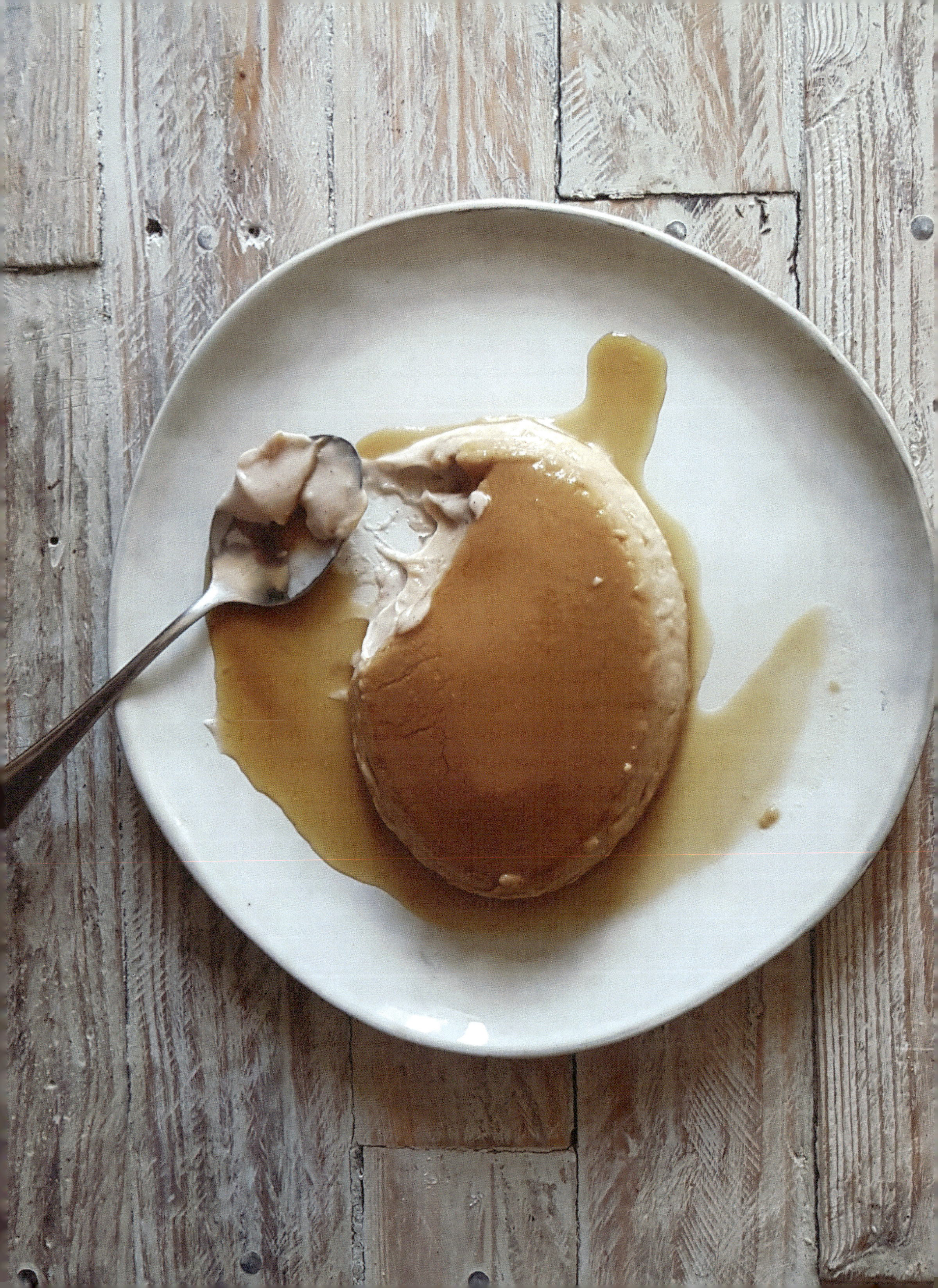

MAMA'S VEGAN FLAN

Serves: 5 | Preperation: 40 Minutes

Flan is a must have in Gibraltar, and there are so many flavours to try: coconut, vanilla, caramel... A smooth and wonderfully set flan is a fabulous way to end a meal. I've put together a vegan alternative for those who don't eat egg, but still want a delicious dessert.

INGREDIENTS

Flan
175ml plant-based milk
300ml full-fat coconut milk
3 tbsp maple syrup
2 tbsp cornstarch
1 tsp agar syrup
2 tsp vanilla extract
½ tsp cinnamon

Caramel*
2 tbsp maple syrup
2 tbsp demerara sugar
½ tsp lemon juice

Or you can use the fudge caramel recipe from page 91 for the caramel layer. Just melt a bit of it in the microwave first, then pour it into the ramekins.

TIME TO FEED THE SOUL

This recipe is in two parts: first the caramel topping and then the flan mixture.

For the caramel: stir the ingredients together in a pan over a medium heat until dissolved. Once smooth, pour this out into 4 ramekins and leave to cool down while you prepare the flan mixture.

Pour the wet ingredients for the flan into a saucepan and stir over a medium heat. Once the mixture is hot, smooth and combined, whisk in the cornstarch.

Continue to stir or whisk until the mixture reduces and thickens. This will happen before it starts to boil.

Once thick, remove the pan from the heat and using a ladle, pour the flan mixture out evenly into the ramekins with the caramel.

Allow the ramekins to cool to room temperature before transferring them to the fridge overnight so that the mixture sets.

When serving, run a knife along the edges of the ramekin and place a plate over the top before flipping it upside down, as the caramel will go everywhere.

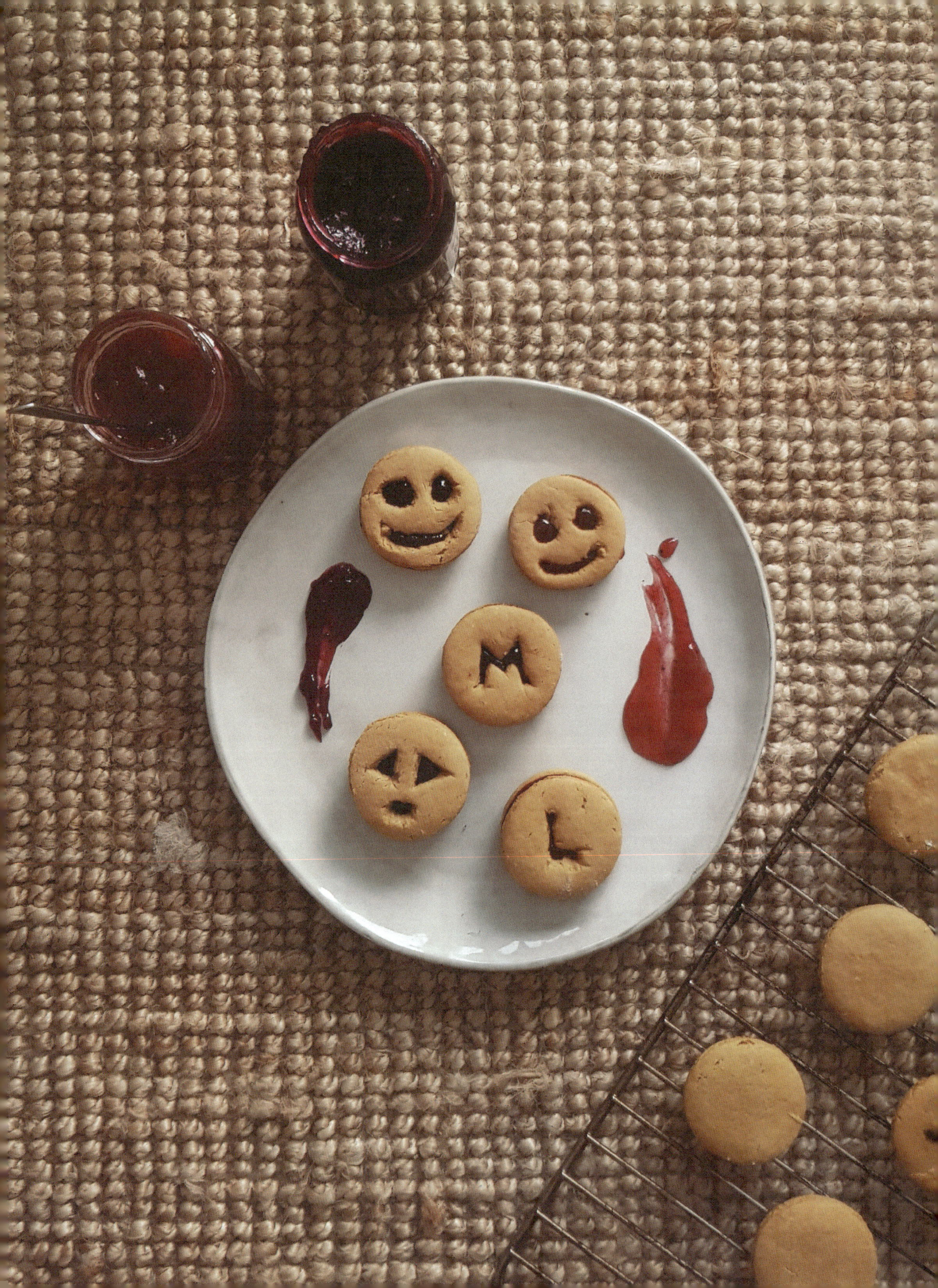

VEGAN JAM BISCUITS

Serves: 4 | Baking Time: 15 Minutes

Who remembers these growing up? Get the kids involved and have some fun in preparing these sticky, sweet, fruit-filled treats. Decorate them however you like, and if you have a cookie cutter then you'll just make your life a lot easier than I did.

INGREDIENTS

- 180g plain flour
- 125g vegan butter
- 60g caster sugar
- 1 tsp vanilla extract
- Your favourite jam

TIME TO FEED THE SOUL

Cream together the butter and sugar, adding in the vanilla extract as you mix.

Once the above is combined and smooth, fold in the flour until you have a crumbly mixture.

Next, use your hands and knead the dough together into a ball. Place the bowl with the dough in the fridge for an hour so that it stiffens up to manipulate later.

When the dough is firmer, preheat the oven to 180°C and lightly flour a clean surface. Roll the dough out with a rolling pin until it's about half a centimetre thick.

Using biscuit cutters, cut out even shapes in equal quantities, then with a smaller cutter or carefully with a sharp knife, cut out a shape in the middle of half of the biscuit shapes, leave the other half untouched.

Lay the biscuits out on a baking tray with a greaseproof paper and bake for 10 - 12 minutes, until they go golden.

When the biscuits have finished baking, allow them to cool off and finally spread a teaspoon of jam on each of the whole biscuits and sandwich them with the shape-cut biscuits.

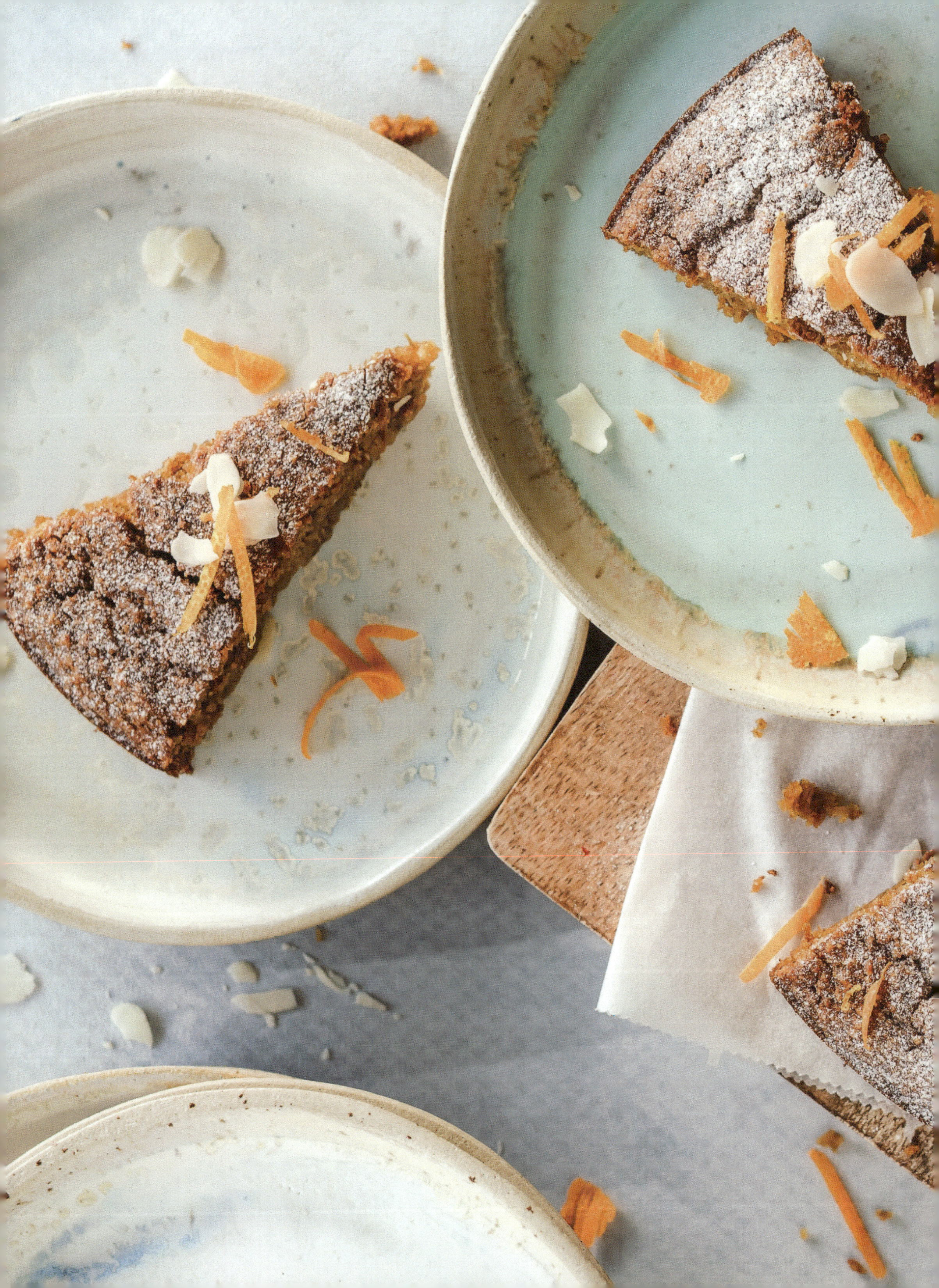

The Cakes

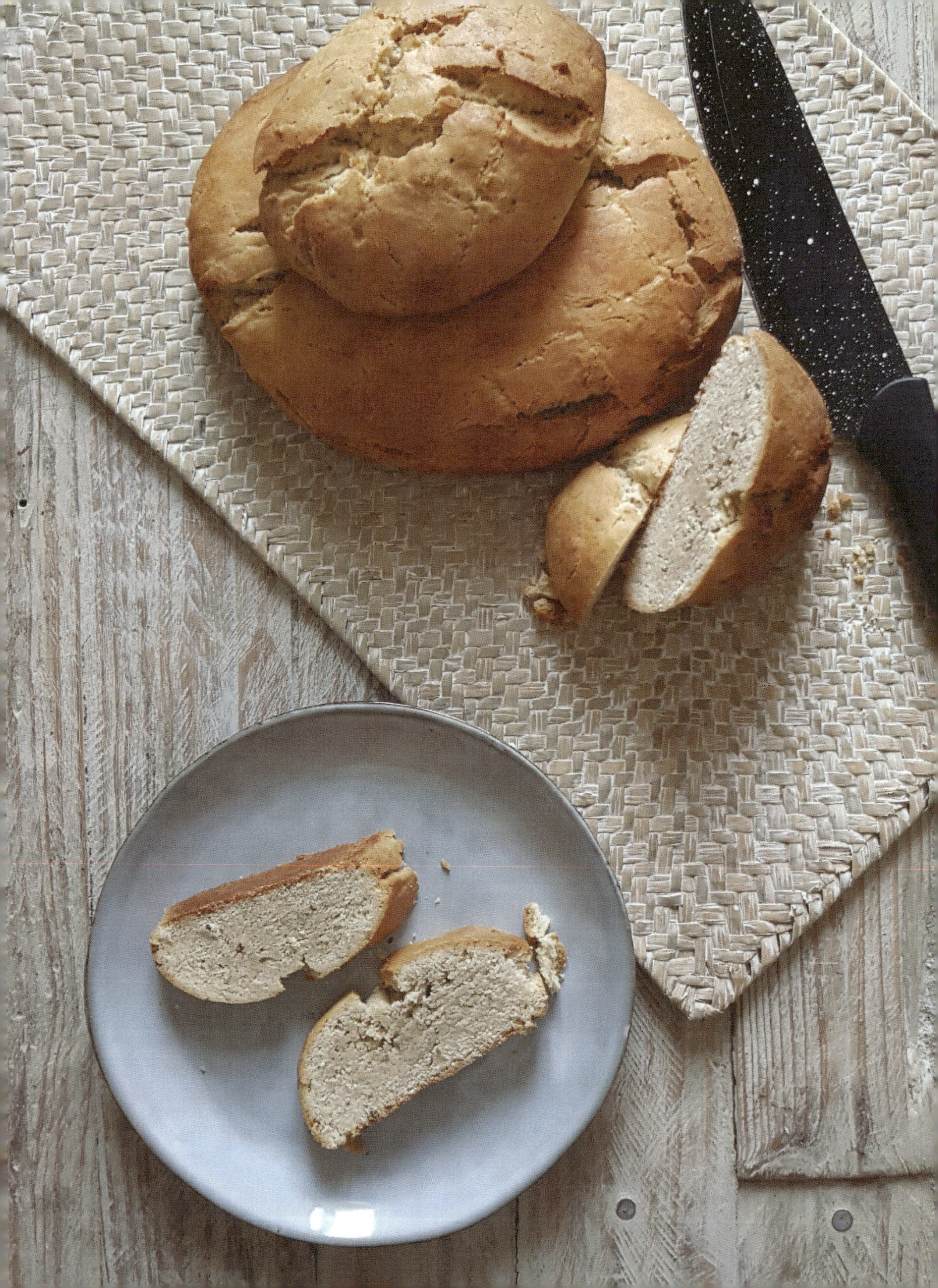

BOLLOS DE HORNAZO

Serves: 5 | Baking Time: 30 Minutes

An Easter staple, the *Bollo de Hornazo* is a must have during the Easter holidays; a traditional tea time favourite. Usually recipe requires many eggs, but I've found a replacement to provide a vegan alternative that doesn't disappoint.

INGREDIENTS

- 700g self-raising flour
- 225g olive oil
- 225g sugar
- 2 bananas
- 2 tbsp aniseed seeds
- Nut milk *(for brushing)*

TIME TO FEED THE SOUL

Preheat the oven to 200ºC

Mash the bananas in a bowl and beat these together with the sugar until smooth and creamy.

Next, add in the olive oil and slowly add the self-raising flour, sieving as you do this. Combine all the ingredients and finally add the aniseed seeds and fold.

Once the dough has formed, sprinkle some flour on your countertop and scoop out the dough onto it. Knead the dough until you can cleanly cut it in half with a knife.

Line a baking tray with greaseproof paper and shape your dough into two large loaves or separate smaller loaves. *(I think smaller loaves works better for this recipe.)* Cut some grooves into the top and brush with some nut milk.

Transfer to the oven and leave to bake for 30 minutes until golden and baked throughout.

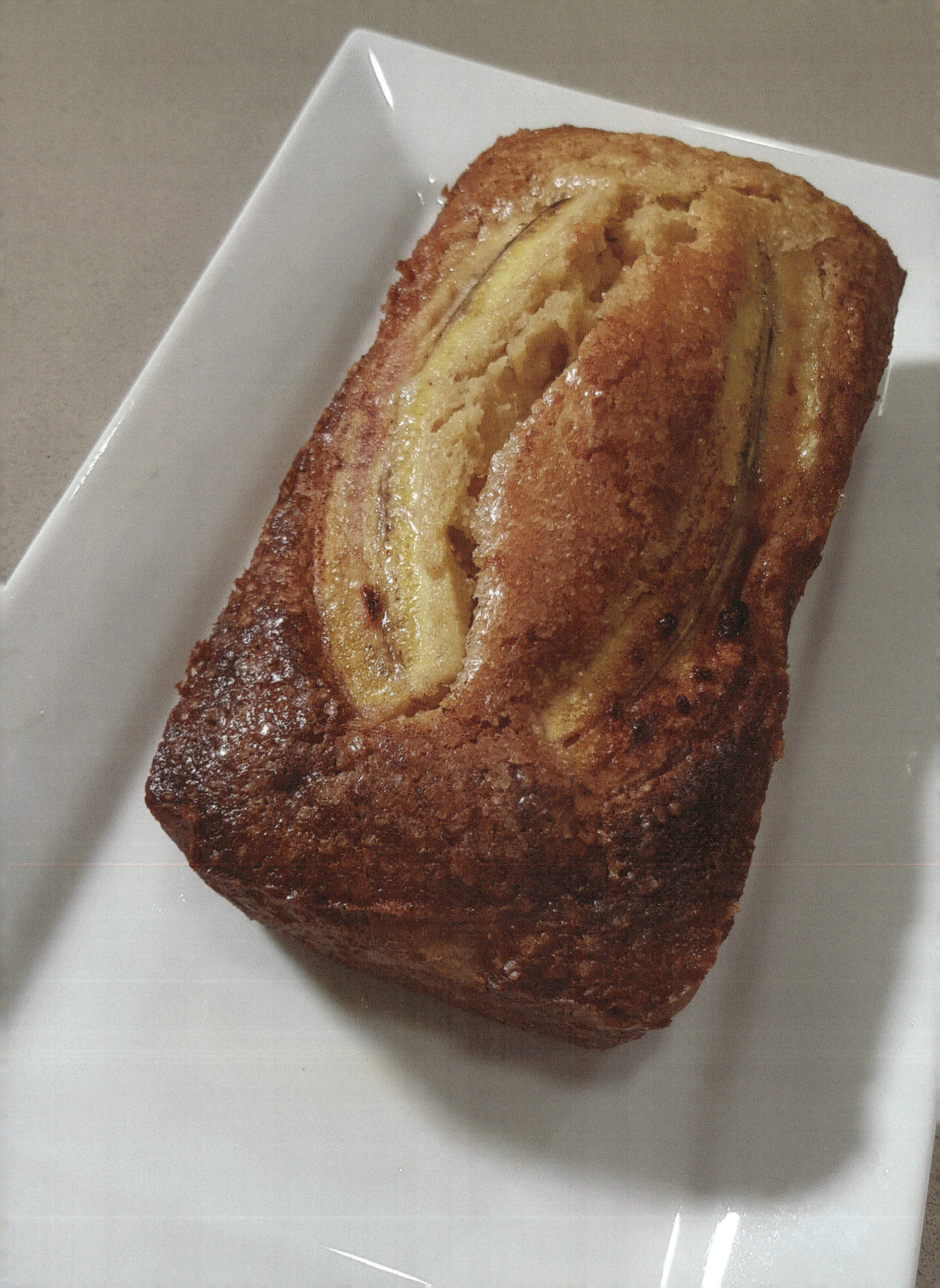

VEGAN BANANA BREAD

Serves: 6 | Baking Time: 1 Hour

Banana bread is great for afternoon tea. This recipe is a nice alternative as we use one of the egg replacements from our grid on page 9 to substitute the egg without affecting the taste. In fact you can play with this by trying applesauce or any other and see what you end up with.

INGREDIENTS

2 tbsp flaxseed
130ml almond milk
2 - 3 very ripe bananas
75g coconut oil
150g demerara sugar
1 tsp vanilla extract
200g self-raising flour
1 tsp baking soda
Pinch of salt

TIME TO FEED THE SOUL

Let's start by making the egg substitute. Mix together the flaxseed and the almond milk. Stir together and let it rest for 2 - 3 minutes - it will start to thicken.

In a separate large bow, mash the banana into a paste. Once you've mixed in the other ingredients, add the flax mixture too and combine everything into a smooth cake mix.

Line a loaf tin with greaseproof paper and pour the mixture in, and finish off by sprinkling a little bit of brown sugar on top. Transfer your tin to the oven and bake for 1 hour. Check to see whether your cake has cooked through by inserting a knife into the middle and checking whether it comes out clean.

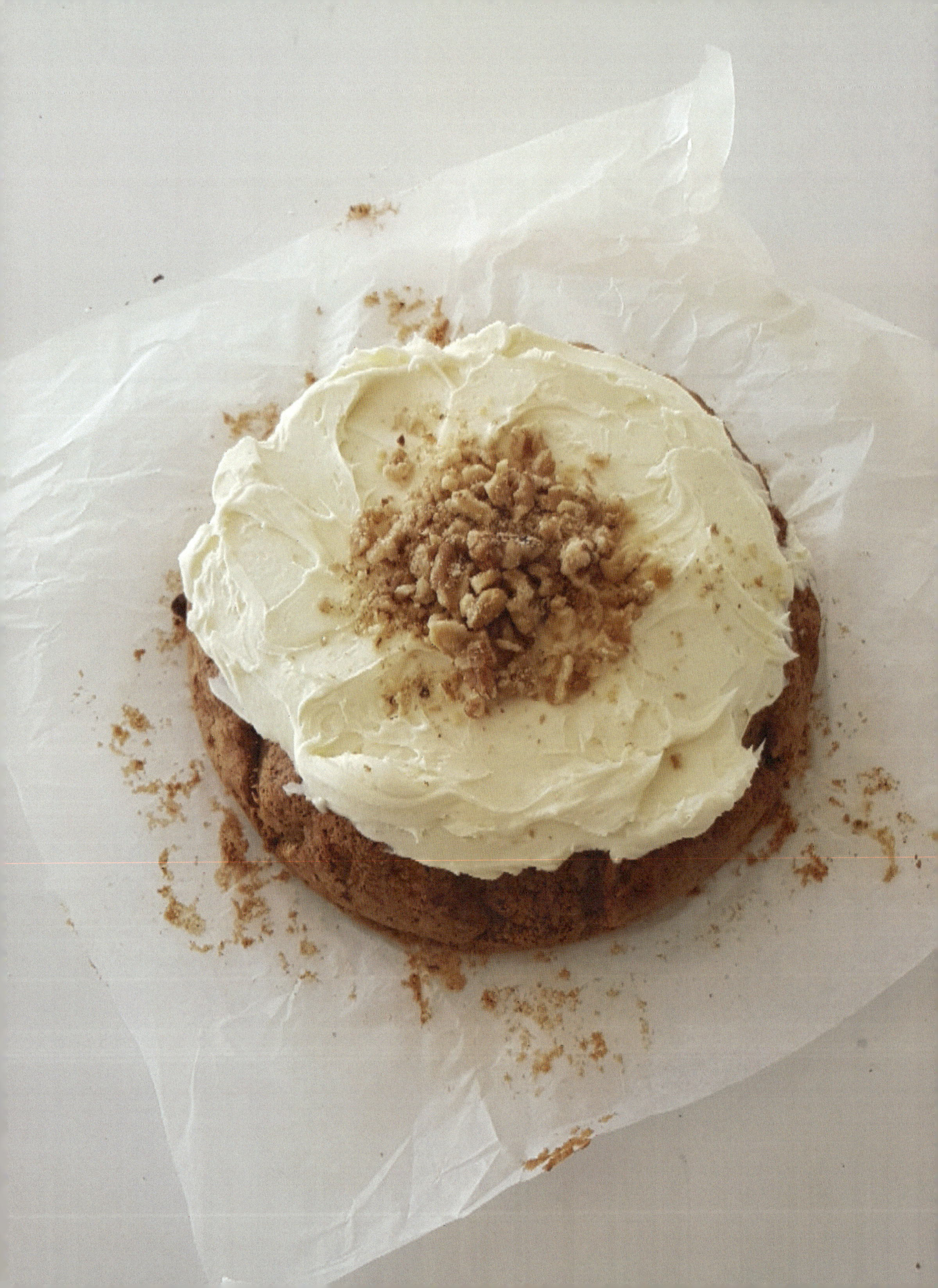

VEGAN CARROT CAKE WITH "CREAM CHEESE"

Serves: 5 | Baking Time: 1 Hour, 10 Minutes

Carrot cake has to be one of, if not definitely, my favourite cake. Making a vegan version was a slight challenge as I tried to get the textures and flavours just right. Sweet and fragrant, heartwarming and filling, just what you'd expect from from this tasty treat.

INGREDIENTS

- 250g plain flour
- 2 tsp baking powder
- 1 tsp ground cinnamon
- 275g brown sugar
- 50g desiccated coconut
- 225ml sunflower oil
- 2 tbsp agave syrup
- 3 tbsp almond milk
- 300g carrots
- 2 tbsp ground flaxseed
- 30g walnuts

Frosting

- 3 tbsp agave syrup
- 200g vegan cream cheese
- Vanilla extract or vanilla bean paste
- 20g walnuts

TIME TO FEED THE SOUL

Preheat the oven to 180ºC.

Start off by preparing your egg replacement. Stir the flaxseed into about 5 tablespoons of tepid water and leave to one side whilst you prepare the rest so that it thickens.

In a large bowl, combine the cinnamon, flour and baking powder together, making sure to sift the ingredients as you do. Add the sugar and coconut and combine everything.

Next add in the oil, agave syrup and almond milk and using a wooden spoon mix everything together so that you have an even mixture.

Grate the carrots, crush the walnuts and add them to the cake mixture along with the now thickened flaxseed mixture and make sure to fold these in evenly.

Spoon the cake mixture into a spring bottom cake tin *(coat the sides of the tin with oil and flour first)*, and bake in the oven for 1 hour 10 minutes or until a knife comes out clean. Once baked let it cool off completely before you add the frosting. *(Trust me, otherwise you will end up with a mess.)*

For the frosting, whisk all the ingredients together *(except for the walnuts)*. Once thick, and the cake is cool, spread it on top of your cake and decorate with the walnuts.

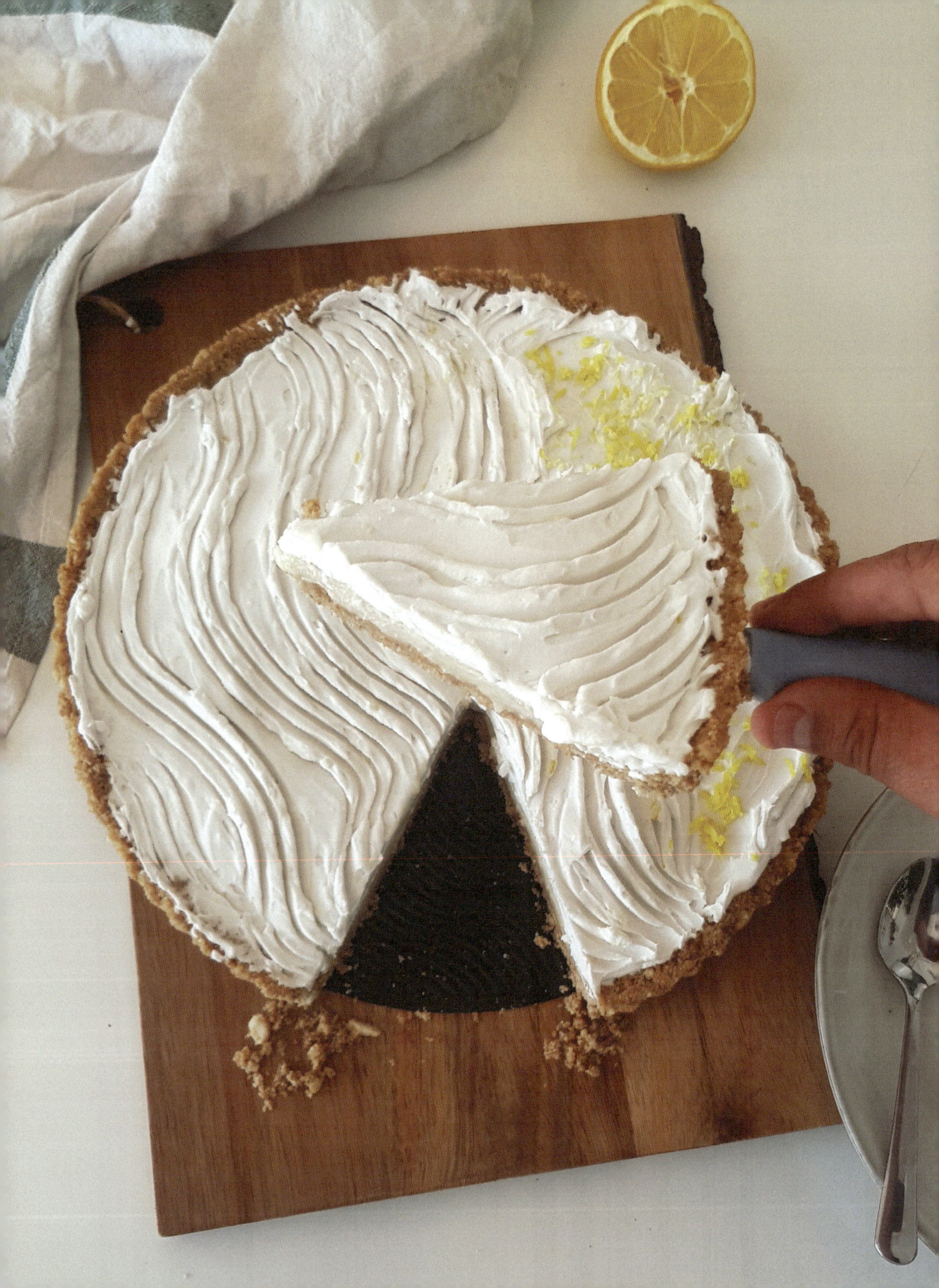

NO BAKE VEGAN LEMON TART

Serves: 6 | Preparation Time: 3 Hours

Add some tang to your day with this guilt-free twist on the classic lemon tart. This dish is especially wonderful to enjoy on hot summer afternoons as a refreshing citrus bite.

INGREDIENTS

Base Crust
- 125g toasted almonds
- 320g vegan digestive biscuits
- ½ tsp cinnamon
- 100ml coconut oil
- 4 tbsp maple syrup

Vegan Lemon Curd
- 175ml lemon juice
- 200ml coconut cream
- 60g caster sugar
- 1 tbsp cornstarch
- 110g maple syrup

Meringue
- 200g thick coconut cream *(two tins)*
- 1 tsp vanilla extract
- 2 tsp icing sugar
- Lemon rind

TIME TO FEED THE SOUL

Start off with the crust. If you have raw almonds then toast them on a hot pan until golden. Place all the dry ingredients in a food processor and crumble until smooth. Once the nuts are broken down into smaller, smoother pieces, pour in the syrup and oil and continue blending until combined.

Transfer the crust mixture into a tart tin and spread evenly. Leave this in the fridge to harden whilst you make the lemon curd.

Next, prepare the lemon curd. Mix all the ingredients together until you have a very smooth mixture; use a whisk for this to achieve the best result. To smoothen out the mixture, whisk in a bowl over a bain-marie to slowly heat the mixture. Once it starts to thicken and turn syrupy, remove from the heat.

When the base has hardened and the curd is thick, pour the curd onto the tart base and place it back in the fridge for 2 - 3 hours until set.

Top the pie with some coconut meringue, which you can make by getting a tin or two of coconut cream and leaving them in the fridge for a few hours before starting. When you open the tins you will find thick white cream on the top layers. Carefully scoop this out leaving the runny liquid behind. Whisk this together with vanilla and sugar and a grating of lemon, then spread this over the curd.

Decorate the top of the tart using your best artistic skills, then leave in the fridge until ready to serve.

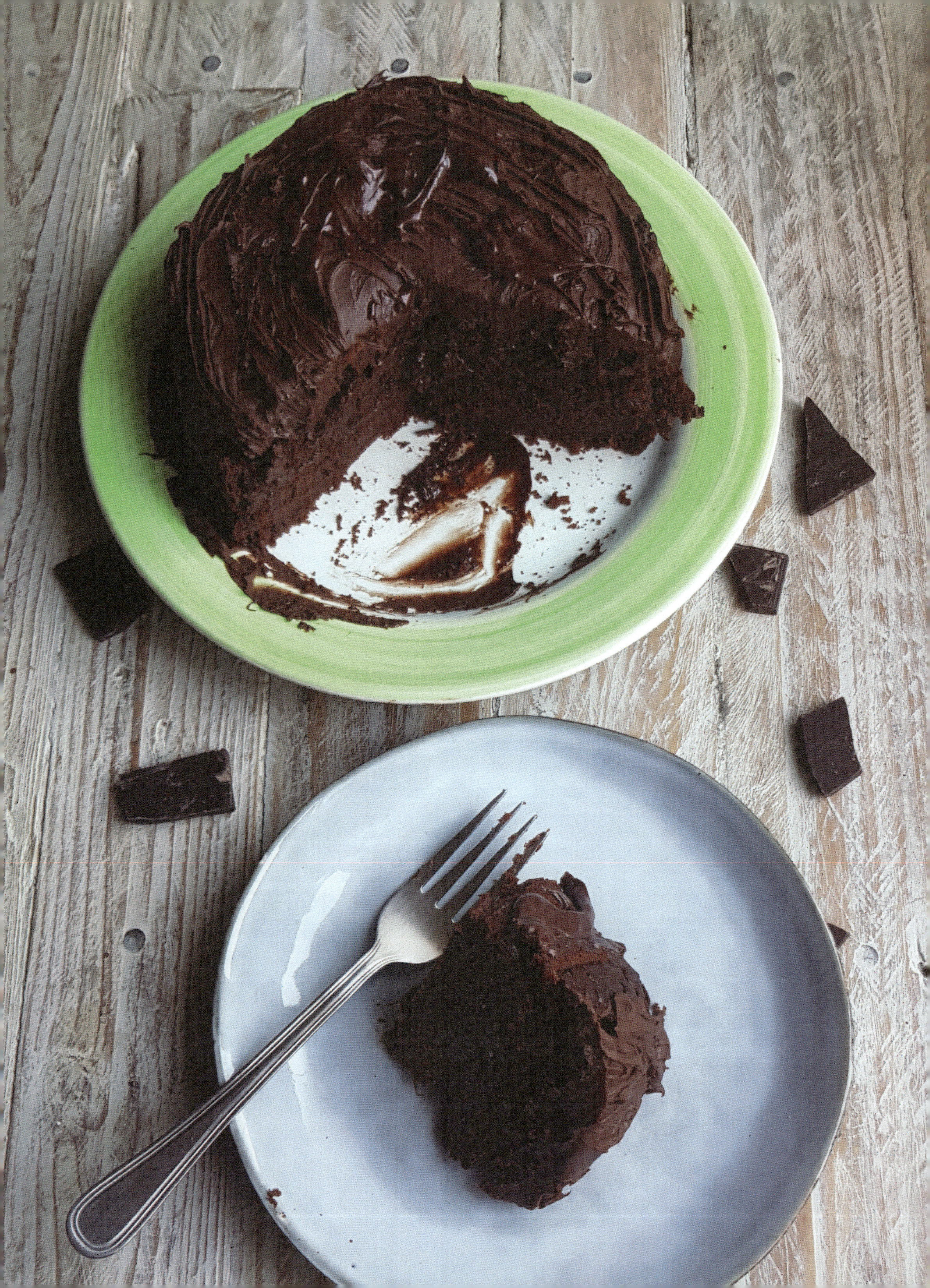

MELT-IN-YOUR-MOUTH CHOCOLATE CAKE

Serves: 6 | Baking Time: 40 minutes

Whether you just want to impress your friends at tea time or prepare something decadent for a birthday, there's always a reason to spoil someone with a chocolate cake.

INGREDIENTS

2 mashed ripe bananas
3 tsp ground flaxseed
1 tsp vanilla extract
2 tbsp peanut butter
180ml maple syrup
100g caster sugar
1 ½ tsp baking powder
60ml plant based milk
125g cocoa powder
320g self raising flour

Chocolate Ganache

120g unsweetened coconut milk
230g dairy-free dark chocolate
115g vegan butter
200g powdered sugar

TIME TO FEED THE SOUL

Preheat your oven to 180ºC.

Mash your bananas and mix them together with the vanilla extract, peanut butter and flaxseed.

Give it a stir and next add the maple syrup, sugar and baking powder and combine, whisking it all together as you add in the milk and cocoa powder and finally self raising flour.

Pour the cake mixture into one large, or two medium, cake tins. Bake in the oven for 40 minutes until a knife comes out clean.

Once ready, remove the cake from the oven and leave to cool. It's time to prepare the ganache whilst the cake cools.

Using the bain-marie method of placing a bowl over a pot of boiling water, heat up the milk. Once hot, add in the chocolate, stirring occasionally to melt it completely.

Once the chocolate has completely melted, remove the bowl from the heat and add the butter, stirring it it into the milk until it melts. Finally, sift in the powdered sugar and whisk it into the mixture until it thickens but remains light and fluffy.

Allow the ganache to cool down in the fridge whilst your cake cools completely. Then layer your cake with the ganache in between (if you used two cake tins) and on top.

(Make sure the cake is completely cooled throughout or it will melt.)

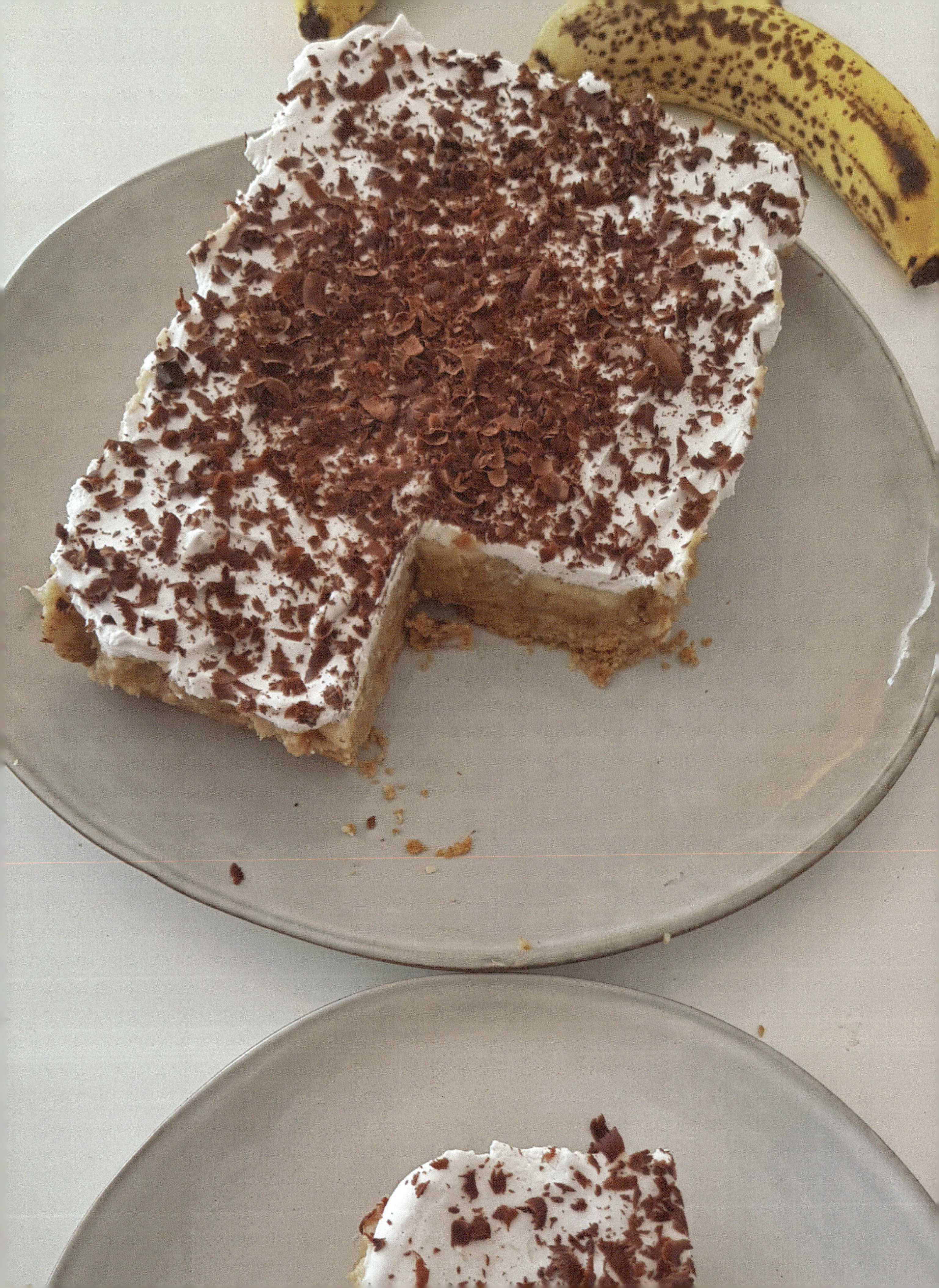

MAMA'S VEGAN BANOFFEE PIE

Serves: 6 | preparation Time: 30 Minutes

Banoffee Pie is one of those classics that reminds me of of family meals out. Sweet toffee and layers of banana over a biscuit base and topped with cream. This recipe is not only dairy-free, but I've managed to get the same taste and consistency using dates, which I never would have thought of before coming up with this recipe.

INGREDIENTS

Base

100g toasted raw almonds

150g vegan digestive biscuits

½ tsp cinnamon

80ml coconut oil

2 tbsp maple syrup

Caramel layer

350g pitted dates

3 Tbsp melted vegan butter

1 tsp lemon juice

1 tsp vanilla bean

3 tbsp maple syrup

2 Bananas

Topping

2 X 400g coconut cream cans

2 large bananas

Dark chocolate

TIME TO FEED THE SOUL

It's important to start this recipe the night before by placing the cans of coconut cream in the fridge so that they stiffen up properly.

Start with the base by placing all the dry ingredients in a food processor and crumbling until smooth. Once the nuts are broken down into smaller, smoother pieces, pour in the syrup and oil and continue blending until everything is thoroughly mixed together.

Transfer the ingredients to a tart tin lined with greaseproof paper and spread evenly. Leave this in the fridge to harden.

Prepare the caramel toffee layer by blending the pitted dates together with the other ingredients until smooth. Pour this on top of the biscuit base and spread evenly.

Slice up 2 bananas into small rounds and place a layer on top of the caramel. Remove the cans of coconut cream from the fridge and scoop out the thick white coconut topping, discarding any liquid.

Beat the thick coconut cream until smooth and silky and spread over the banana and caramel layer. Finally, shave some dark chocolate over everything and serve.

MAMA LOTTIES
·GIBRALTAR'S RECIPE WEBSITE·

WWW.MAMALOTTIES.COM

Printed in Great Britain
by Amazon